FEASTING

FEASTING

WITH

BOMPAS & PARR

Sam Bompas & Harry Parr

Special photography by Beth Evans and Nathan Pask

PAVILION

CONTENTS

INTRODUCTION   6

FEASTING SINCE THE DAWN OF TIME   12

THEMES   20

TABLE DRESSING   24

MAGIC & FOOD   28

FLOWERS   33

EXPLOSIVES AT DINNER   36

SERVICE & UNIFORMS   44

PLANNING   48

RECIPES   50

    CANAPÉS   52

    SOUPS & STARTERS   70

    MAINS   88

        FISH   90

        FOWL   94

        MEAT   100

    DESSERT   112

    AFTER DINNER   140

    COCKTAILS   156

    MY LOVE LETTER TO CHAMPAGNE TOWERS

    BY FIONA LEAHY   180

    THE MORNING AFTER   182

    ACCOMPANIMENTS   196

INDEX   216

SUPPLIERS   222

BIBLIOGRAPHY & SALUTE   223

INTRODUCTION

Food is fun. It is a sensual pleasure that everyone can enjoy together, in groups of eight to thirty-three thousand, following the recipes in this book.

Creating a gastronomic sensation doesn't have to be complex. You needn't feast off slow-cooked, obscure cuts of meat from the deer you shot yourself to have a hugely enjoyable meal. This book illustrates how ordinary food and ordinary spaces can be used in such extraordinary ways to make feasting a joy for everyone sitting down.

While neither of us have had any formal culinary training we've found that with the right approach, hard work, grit and imagination the mundane can be magical. Jellies can glow in the dark, the Sunday roast turns into a work of art with big and nasty flavours, and the front room becomes the lost city of Atlantis.

You can do this too without much difficulty. Scattered throughout the book are our hot tips and hard-learnt techniques for creating the ultimate feast. It's a treasure hunt to track them down. You may not be Cordon Bleu trained by the end, but hopefully you will understand what really impresses people when they sit down for a party meal.

At Bompas & Parr we set off on our own food adventures in 2007. Since then we have hosted a jelly banquet for 2,000 people, built the Architectural Punch Bowl where a Grade 1 listed building was flooded with enough alcoholic punch to boat across, created a Ziggurat of Flavour where visitors got their five a day through their lungs and eyeballs, and made a flavour changing gum with 40,000 potential aromas.

We've cooked and organized feasts spread over three miles where every guest changed place every course, another based on dirt at Southeast London's Crossness pumping station, a Victorian temple to sewage and explored the culinary implications of science fiction and the food of the future.

Many of the secrets, ideas, recipes and inspirations behind our feasts are explored in this book. Even without any formal chefs training you too can create epic feasts that amaze, beguile and enchant. This is not so much a cookbook but an adventure story that happens to be true.

Along the way we'll look at the impact of interiors on taste, drinks that would impress even Oliver Reed, pirate party drugs, food on all fours and how to get meaty with medieval dishes. We'll even have a look at the cocktails of satanist Aleister Crowley, meat jewellery and how to make exotic candies.

The recipes in this book are all our own, except those that we have plagarized from other volumes, parents, lovers and the internet. Rest assured, we have only stolen from the best to present dishes that will change your approach to feasting. Read the book all the way through and let's explore this strange and fascinating field – the realm of the epic meal.

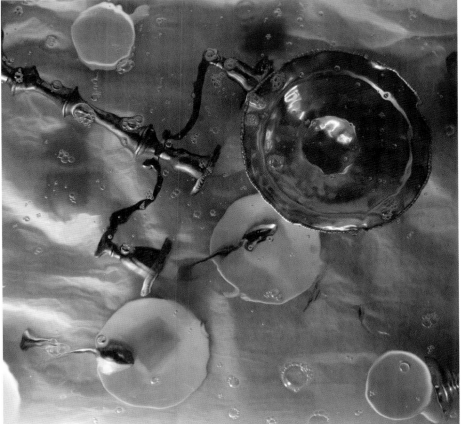

Page 5: A recreation of the 300-dish dessert banquet served to Elizabeth I in 1575 at Kenilworth Castle, including dessert sausages (rice pudding in pig's intestines) and sugar sculptures.

Page 7: Go meaty or go home... Sam and Harry as barbarians in front of their historic Ziggurat of Flavour. Portrait by fantasy artists, Julie Bell and Boris Vallejo.

Opposite (top): This ice sculpture was hacked apart to chill down cocktails in the Masonic Temple of Andaz Hotel.

Opposite (below): Architectural neon jellies (St Paul's Cathedral and Buckingham Palace).

Above: Massed cutlery – a charming and functional sideboard display.

Left: Submerged supper, featuring the peach and green chartreuse jellies served for the last supper on the Titanic in 1912.

Overleaf: Dinner in a sewage plant. The exotic location somehow made a menu exploring the culinary implications of dirt more palatable.

FEASTING SINCE THE DAWN OF TIME

We're always inspired by grand historical feasts. Here are some of the most savage, outrageous and awesome meals since the dawn of time. They may not be the most sensible meals but they're certainly sensational, so get stuck in:

11. SAVOY GONDOLA BANQUET (1905)

At the turn of the nineteenth century George Kessler flooded the forecourt of the Savoy Hotel in London for a banquet. They populated the flooded room with fish and swans, but there was so much dye in the water that the animals were accidentally poisoned. The walls of the dining room were painted with dioramas of Venice and the meal was served to guests in a silk-lined gondola illuminated by 400 Venetian lamps and decorated with 12,000 carnations. The dessert was served from the back of a baby elephant, which marched up the gangplank.

10. THE ROMAN ORGY (218-222)

Heliogabalus was famous for his passion for cruel jokes and his party guests were frequently reminded of this. At one of the Roman emperor's events, grains of gold were mixed in peas, and rubies and pearls were placed in other dishes throughout the meal.

The guests kept the jewels but not all of their teeth. An additional trick he would play on his guests is after the large feasts they would go to their bedrooms, so Heliogabalus would lock them in the dining space and let in his own declawed lions and bears. This often ended in fatalities.

9. FRANÇOIS MITTERRAND'S LAST SUPPER (1996)

The former French President François Mitterrand decided when he was dying to stop taking medication and concentrate on his last meal. This consisted of two dozen oysters, capon in cream and roasted ortolan, the tiny songbird that is consumed whole in one large single bite.

This is quite an undertaking and not just because of the size and awkwardness of the mouthful. The endangered bird is illegal and with good reason. Ortolan are captured alive before their eyes are poked out to disrupt their eating habits. They are then force-fed oats and millet until they are four times their natural size before they are killed by drowning in Armagnac.

The eating process is to place the entire roasted bird in one's mouth with just the beak protruding, and then slowly chew it for about 15 minutes. You are supposed to

Above: The Gondola Banquet at the Savoy Hotel, London, in 1905. The poisoned fish and swans are missing from this photo!

experience: first the rich taste of fat and brandy, then the bitterness of the bird's guts, and finally the crunchy bones lacerating your gums - the blood from your gums adds to the flavour. It is traditional to cover your head and face with a napkin when chewing on your ortolan. The napkin is used, depending on who you believe, either to keep the delicate aromas in, or to hide from God. Mitterrand ate two for his last supper.

8. DINING AT THE ZOO (1870)

Paris was under siege. In response to the food crisis Monsieur Bonvalet, the mayor of a Parisian district, held a feast. His solution was to make use of the city's zoo and fill the nutritional gap with wild animals. Bonvalet

invited 20 guests to a dinner at Noel Peters' restaurant. The meal consisted of "English-style" elephant, bear meat roasted in a pepper sauce, and camel.

7. THE DESCENDING TABLE (1750)

Louis XV mistress Madame Pompadour hosted a *petit souper*. Little was reported on the meal itself but the hostess received very high praise. Madame Pompadour wished to avoid any communication or awkwardness between the guests and the servants, and she achieved this by setting the meal in a dining room with a trap door. After each course the table descended through an opening in the floor to be laid with new tableware and food.

6. HORSES ON THE SKYSCRAPER (1903)

The millionaire C.K.G. Billings held a feast for the Equestrian club of New York at the top of a skyscraper. Billings brought 32 horses up to Louis Sherry's restaurant in the lift. The guests ate on horseback – pheasant from feed bags and champagne from rubber casks. The idea behind the feast was a democratic celebration whereby the horse should also be rewarded by dinner.

5. HELL BANQUET (1511)

In 1511, dining group The Company of the Trowel held their notorious Hell Banquet. They were a gang of respected artists and hosted by Leonardo da Vinci on a number of occasions. On arrival, guests were invited by Pluto to join him in the underworld for his wedding feast to Proserpina. Entering through the gaping mouth of Hades, jaws of a huge serpent, hinged to open and close for each couple in turn, guests found themselves in a circular room, gloomily lit by one small candle. A devil with a pitchfork showed them to their places at a black draped table, while their host declaimed that the torments of Hell would be suspended for the time being in honour of his wedding. About the walls of the room were pictured the "holes" of the damned, their tortures periodically revealed by "flames", which could be made to flare up beneath them.

Food was in the guise of repulsive creatures ostensibly serpents, lizards, toads, newts, spiders, frogs, scorpions and the like; actually the deceptive exteriors concealed delicious titbits. Service of such dishes came on a fire shovel, while wine was poured by a "devil" from an ugly sort of rhyton into drinking cups that were actually glass-melting ladles. Skeleton bones made of sugar and marzipan formed the dessert course.

| **Above:** C.K.G. Billings' horseback dinner at Sherry's, 1903.

4. WHITE HOUSE CHEESE FEST (1836)

The seventh president Andrew Jackson hosted frequent public benders at the White House and the most epic centred on a vast cheese. In 1835 dairy farmer, Thomas Meacham presented Old Hickory with a 635 kg/1,400 lb wheel of cheese. The cheese was left to ferment for a year. When it was good and ripe Jackson took out a nationwide advertisement in the papers as an invitation to the public to help him eat the cheese. Apparently the cheese could be smelt within a half mile radius of the White House. Ten thousand members of the public attended the president's final public party and it took two hours to devour the cheese.

3. POLITICS IN PARIS (1901)

In a bid to threaten the power of the Parisian city government the French president Émile Loubet, a former mayor, held a party for 20,000 people. In order to cook this vast amount of food, 12 additional temporary kitchens had to be built. The quantity of produce was extraordinary; the feast included 2268 kg/5,000 lb of beef, 2722 kg/6,000 lb of salmon, 2,500 ducks, 2,500 chickens, 1,500 pheasants, 33,000 bottles of wine and 7,000 bottles of champagne. The 3,000 waiters servicing the tables had to ride bicycles to get the food out hot.

| **Above:** The Royal Pavilion in Brighton, the site of Carême's greatest triumph.

2. CARÊME'S ARCHITECTURAL SUGAR (1817)

The great chef Antonin Carême is one of our absolute heros. Carême was known as the "king of chefs and chef to kings" and variously cooked for Napoleon, George IV and Tsar Alexander.

He drew inspiration from buildings, claiming that architecture's main branch was confectionery. Carême made his name with 2-m/6-ft high *pièce montées* (mounted pieces), elaborate table decorations that represented rotundas, temples, columns and arches in varied Classical, Gothic and Chinoiserie styles. He was so successful he could afford to turn down a permanent job offer from Tsar Alexander I.

His major impact on cuisine came through the invention of the *toque* (chef's hat), extraordinary sauces and dishes and through importing *service à la Russe* (how we eat now) to Europe from the Russian court. Carême drew a direct line between food and architecture. His great works of pastry and confectionery were directly inspired by buildings. While working in Russia he spent his spare time working on the book *Projects for the Architectural Embellishment of St Petersburg*. For the publication he toured the public spaces of the city and made notes of areas that to his confectioner's eye could do with some "embellishment".

The Prince Regent (later to become George IV) invited Carême to create a feast served at the Royal Pavilion in Brighton. George had the chief create 127 dishes and most impressive feature of the night was a 1.21-m/4-ft Turkish mosque created entirely out of marzipan.

1. NEOPOLITAN *CUCCAGNA* MONUMENT – A FOOD MOUNTAIN (1747)

Cuccagna monuments formed the centrepieces for the most spectacular public feasts in history. They are vast architectural structures made of food. Following a grand display, the mountainous monument would be entirely consumed by the public in a sustained bout of savage civic eating.

The monuments drew inspiration from the mythical "Land of Cockaigne", a fabled paradise on Earth and popular tale among medieval peasants (Spencer; 1998). It is a bounteous world centred on food where no one goes hungry, grows old or works hard. There are rivers of wine, mountains made of cheese, rainstorms of cakes and sweets (candies), and the wildlife is precooked and desperate to be eaten. Life presents itself as easy, full of sensual pleasures and without responsibility. People eat, play games, occasionally visit the fountain of youth and the only punishment is for those who try to work too hard.

In Naples in the eighteenth century Cockaigne's spirit of plenty was embodied by a procession of food carts and chanting peasants. The festivities climaxed when the central square was reached and the produce was piled into a huge food mountain. When the king gave the signal, the masses were allowed to descend on the mountain and take what they liked.

This festival evolved to become much more artistic with leading architects and artists engaged to create vast landscapes, gardens and buildings entirely out of food in high baroque style. Vincenzo dal Re's *Cuccagna* for the birth of Charles VI in 1747 is a formal garden with large central fountain flowing with wine and overlooked by an epic arcaded structure made of edibles. The mountain paths and balustrades were made of *caciocavallo* cheese and the arcades clad with meat.

Our Ziggurat of Flavour was directly inspired by *Cuccagna* monuments of yore.

Cuccagna monuments also featured greased poles surmounted with fowl. Local teams would compete to scale the pole and claim a triumphal bird. Party on!

Below: On his days off Carême would pop down to the library to sketch architectonic desserts.

Vincenzo Re inv. e dis.

Cuccagna posta sulla Piazza del

A. Casino coperto di Lardo, Panzette, Presciutti, : Balaustri di Cacio Cavallo. : Capre, Palombi, e Galline. D. Due stili sopra de quali due
Cacio cotto vecchio Cavallo, e Pane Sopressate, B. Monte con tre strade coperto di Cacio Ca- C. Peschiera con Papere, ed Anatre, ti da Foretano, uno da Uomo, e
Galline, Papere, Galli d'India, e Palombi, con vallo, e Cacio di Morea, Pecore, Bovi, Porci, con varie sorti di Pesce. da Donna tutti guarniti d'

XI

18

Giuseppe Vasi incise

l Palazzo
ana di vino.   H. Parter tutto coperto di Caci d'ogni   ne, Presciutti, Cacio Cavallo,   M. Parte della Chiesa di
ana d'acqua.   genere, Presciutti, e Pane.   ed altro di diversa qualità   S. Fran.° di Paola.
e di vino.   I. Piedestalli, e Vasi composti di Pa-   L. Lazzari che corrono a dare il Sacco   N. Spezieria di S. Spirito.

Left: Vincenzo dal Re's 1747 *Cuccagna*, from *Narrazione delle Solemni Reali Feste*, engraved by Giuseppe Vasi. The peasants are about to tuck in...

THEMES

Harry's hair is going grey and he's not even 30. We spend weeks and months not sleeping, the next event closing in and a creeping terror rising. Fear is the goad to creativity and helps us put in the hours of work needed to achieve the extraordinary.

Feasting is all about impressing your guests. Spectacle is just as important as the food itself. Don't get us wrong - what people put in their mouths has to be good. It's just that most folk are far more visually literate than they are in terms of the odours, textures and tastes that compose a mouthful of food. This is well illustrated by truffles. Physicist and flavour expert Dr Len Fisher points out that "a full 40 percent of the population are 'tone deaf' to the core odours in truffles that gourmets rave about." But most people go wild for a truffled dish.

These days we typically only spend 20 per cent of project time on the food. The rest is used to engineer other ways to impress. A good strong theme is an excellent place to begin.

Choosing a theme can be tricky. The wrong creative direction will leave you looking infantile, puerile or perverse. Handily there are a few methods that deliver hot results. Though the golden age of feasting is over, history provides a rich seam of inspiration to mine. The elements and ideas that rocked the best parties, orgies and bachanals of earlier civilizations will probably still be effective today. We detail some of the greatest feasts in history on p.10-17. The application of powerful modern techniques and technologies to these ancient practices will yield results that delight and amaze.

One example that we found particularly inspiring, and re-created for our culinary adventure *The Complete History of Food*, took place on New Year's Eve, 1853.

You should take all opportunities to impress and amaze, and this epic feast did so from the start by printing invitations on replica pterodactyl wings. Enough information was given to intrigue guests, get them to the right place, and leave them hungry to find out more.

It read:

Mr. B. Waterhouse Hawkins solicits the honour of Professor (XXXXX)'s company at dinner, in the Iguanodon, on the 31st of December, 1853, at 4 p.m.

When the guests arrived, they were not disappointed. Anatomist Richard Owen, an expert on dinosaurs (he invented the word itself), had teamed up with sculptor Benjamin Waterhouse Hawkins to create 33 life-size model dinosaurs at Crystal Palace. This was the first time anyone had attempted to build

> "ANXIETY IS THE HANDMAIDEN OF CREATIVITY."
> – T. S. ELIOT –

| **Above:** Here's an etching of the original Iguanodon Banquet from the *Illustrated London News*.

scale models of dinosaurs, neatly combining showmanship, art and science. In celebration, Hawkins invited Owen and 20 other scientists to dine *inside* the giant model iguanodon.

The feast followed seven formidable courses, all served by a team of waiters who had to clamber over scaffolding-supported platforms to reach the diners. It started with a choice of mock turtle, Julien or hare soup and finishing with a bountiful array of fruits and nuts, going through fish, game and sweet courses in between, all washed down with large quantities of alcohol.

According to the *Illustrated London News*, the party left "well pleased with the modern hospitality of the iguanodon" and Hawkins, their raucous singing was comparable to a herd of bellowing iguanodons. The next day, the papers noted that if the diners had been born in ancient times, they would have been the meal in the creature's belly.

You could trust your instincts and go with the first thing that comes into your head. To ensure that you have an original idea you can always combine themes employing a random "dot cricket" method to produce more unusual titles like "Renaissance Swamp" or "Noah's Ark in Space". Note down a load of places, objects, emotions, eras you think will be fun and randomly put a few together. The results can be grand. One of our more successful parties was held at Harry's house with the theme Halloween Harrods. Harry's woodchip-papered stairwell is still gold and covered in hieroglyphics. One guest wore nothing but a small Harrods bag from the perfume counter. it was so tight he brought a spare, in case he needed the loo!

When you've chosen a theme explore all the sensory implications using visuals, sounds and smells for a full frontal sensory assault. This is what we did for the Jelly Banquet in UCL's (University College London's) neoclassical quad. You could say that the theme was architecture meets jelly. For multisensory stimulation hundreds of architectural jellies quivered in a synchronized jelly dance to a soundscape of wobbling jelly recorded in UCL's anechoic chamber by sound artist Douglas Murphy and Professor of Biophysics Jonathan Ashmore. Jelly dancers pranced around with massive spoons in costumes from a lingerie designer and non-stop strawberry aroma wafted through the buildings. The night culminated in jelly wrestling and the London's greatest jelly fight.

The key is to choose something you and your friends will enjoy and commit to the hilt, missing no opportunity to amaze, inspire and delight.

Right: Our library is a grand source of inspiration.
Opposite: Here you can see the decapitated head of our iguanodon from *The Complete History of Food* where it is today – strapped to the wall of our studio. It looms above Harry's desk.

PUS
PIRATICAL GIN VE

ERRIS' ETHER BAR

TABLE DRESSING

Once you've nailed the theme for your feast, have a think about the space where people will eat and what they'll dine off. Our favourite academic paper was published in 2003 by Professor John Edwards. His team at Bournemouth University found that the same dish, chicken à la king (a creamy beige slop), tasted different, depending on the environment in which it was eaten. This is the dish tipped over Tom Cruise's head in *Cocktail*. For Prof. Edward's meal it was tasted in ten different locations, including a school, a care home, an Army base and a swanky restaurant. The more salubrious the surroundings, the higher the score: in the posh joints, it was rated as moist, tasty and filling, while in one of the dives, it was perceived to be claggy, dry and disgusting. So every item surrounding the meal, decorative or otherwise, will actually add to the meal.

If you eat in a space that looks magical, with fancy table dressing, the food and drink will be awesome - or at least you won't notice that it's grim. The people who eat at the Pirate's Dinner Adventure in Orlando, Florida, don't worry how "Pillager's Pork" or "Treasure's Chicken" comes, because they're eating in front of a fully rigged pirate galleon and being served by wenches.

You do not necessarily need a pirate galleon spectacle. There are plenty of cheap options using items you probably already own or can easily obtain that can help achieve a similar effect. One good example of this - that has subsequently come back to haunt us - is the use of jam jars as exotic glassware. We own about 3,000 jam jars as they are so cheap (more so than hiring glasses) and have used them as wine glasses for Alice in Wonderland meals and as table dressings containing lurid fluids, strange beetles, geodes and incense burning candles. If you mass up enough jam jars with weird objects down the centre of the table it looks convincing. In fact, any object repeated in vast numbers to form a pattern can look enchanting.

We've now used jam jars so much we see them as the closest thing to a poison chalice but they have seen us through a lot. They represent a fine example of a simple and cheap trick that can be much more effective than the expensive alternatives.

Not only does a container load of jam jars provide matching glassware for huge numbers of people, but they add to the experience, immediately giving a surreal edge to proceedings and leaving guests wondering what the next surprise will be. The fact they might not be as functional as their traditional counterpart only serves to heighten

the experience – you can't take yourself too seriously drinking from a jam jar, especially when you and those around you have spilled half the contents, so social boundaries are broken down as well. They also make excellent cocktail shakers in an emergency.

Another hot favourite, that we still realize whenever we have the chance, is the liberal use of pigs' heads and/or trotters. These prize cuts are not sold in supermarkets, but don't worry that's to your advantage. It'll be novel for guests as well as transporting them back to the golden days of medieval feasting. And again they're cheap for you, as the butchers can't sell them. For £5 there's a pig's head in the middle of a table which really makes a statement – it cannot be ignored or fail to be talked about. Pig's heads are such a large chunk of flesh that however long you slam them in the oven for there's always a piece

that's perfectly cooked somewhere in there. The cooked trotters make effective, if greasy, cigarette holders. A bar snack to go with the nicotine fix.

The food itself can be used as a decorative element. Go medieval and mound whatever you've cooked into great piles to decorate the tables. Serving any food this way is called *en pyramide*. Go for quality in your courses and quantity with the table decorations (edible or otherwise). Choose ingredients that are cheap per volume, like popcorn, and stack it up – this becomes popcorn *en pyramide*, the Frenchified name adding a gloss of sophistication to the spectacle. Fruit, ribs and doughnuts are effective too. And there's no need to keep your pudding in the fridge till the last course – why not use it to set the table? Gently wobbling jellies are a joy on any table.

One other dimension to consider with table décor is the getting the right amount of height. Too much height in the decorations and centrepieces and you won't be able to have a conversation across the table, too little and the décor will feel anaemic. Apparently candles should be cut to height so they don't dazzle they eyes but are still tall enough to illuminate the cleavage.

If you get the opportunity, you can simply gild everything you can get your hands on and lay it down the centre of the table, creating a feast for kings. If you can't spare the gold (E number 175 – best bought from a builders merchant like Leyland), grab some gold spray paint, or any other colour for that matter. You can then create an infinite number of matching table decorations, gathered from charity shops but creating the impression of vast opulence. Collect broken and neglected porcelain figurines, plastic toys, alcohol miniatures, weird 1970s furnishings, cheap fake flowers and spray them with your considered colour palette for the evening (eg Fox's party ring colours, elephant's breath blue). If you go with a designated range of colours for the evening's table dressing, lighting and service the results will be much punchier.

Monochrome meals have a glorious if debauched history too. A favourite feast of ours is Grimod de la Reynière's Black Banquet in 1783. Invitations were sent, bordered in black, like funeral notices, to 300 guests, (only 22 to dine – the rest would observe the spectacle as per usual 18th-century practice).

As a testament to how good the invitations were, Louise XVI is said have framed one.

On arrival, guests were questioned by a sentry who asked if they were to be to be received by M. de la Reynière "oppressor of the people" or M. de la Reynière "defender of the people". They continued to pass through a series of rooms, being greeted and/or challenged by men in chain mail and choirboys, burning funeral incense. Finally they entered a dark, candlelit room where the table had a catafalque (coffin holder) as a centrepiece, while each guest had their own coffin placed behind their chair by way of a place marker.

So, the key is to dress your table with abandon. Guests confronted with piles of fruits, trotters, jellies, pigs' heads on sticks and perhaps a few mirrored runners to double the amount of food apparent (mirrored Perspex is more affordable than glass), will toast you as king or queen of the feast.

Page 25: Gild everything you can get your hands on for an opulent table display.
Right: Massed tea lights in jam jars – cheap but effective,
Opposite: We look to Fiona Leahy Design for table dressing inspiration. Here's her take on gold.

MAGIC & FOOD

Since the dawn of time food and magic have been intertwined. There are references to magic in the ancient Egyptian Westcar Papyrus dating back to 2,000 BC. It talks about the marvels performed at the court of King Cheops where a magician by the name of Dedi is thought to have beheaded animals before re-attaching the heads and bringing them back to life. These performances culminated in the grandest feasts.

Some of the best Biblical "tricks" and miracles involve spectacular food performances - like feeding the 5,000. Jesus managed to satisfy multitudes with five loaves and two fish. It's a savvy approach to spreading the good word and impressing hungry followers. The miracle touches the most impressionable organ, the belly, and so everyone can relate.

Magical practices have contributed to a general improvement in the variety and wonder of what we can put in our stomachs today. Alchemists probing the mysteries of the occult failed to find the philosopher's stone but managed to transform base wines into powerful spirits - the raw ingredients for today's cocktail culture.

Before cracking into how magic is playing a key role at today's best tables and can assist at yours it might help to clarify what we mean by the term. Magic by definition, can be many things. Jonathan Allen, magic circle member and curator of the Hayward Gallery's travelling show *Magic* advised us to differentiate between the occult or esoteric tradition and stage conjuring. The former incorporates black magic, wizardry and witchcraft with practitioners purporting to possess arcane and ancient power, possibly with a supernatural origin. Stage magicians and conjurors will readily admit that their power comes from well-practiced sleight of hand, psychology and maybe science. That's not to say they won't confound and mystify, but they do so with the goal of entertainment.

In recent years Michelin-starred restaurants have shifted the relationship between diner and chef to that of audience and stage magician. You go to be enchanted and bewildered rather than fed. Dishes fizz, crackle and smoke as they are cooked with novelty nitrogen cold, the texture and form of foods are transformed and manipulated with chemicals like methyl cellulose and gellan gum, and the waiter rips into a magician's patter as he serves your dinner. It's worth bearing this in mind when preparing your own feast. There's a lot that can be learnt from magicians and their approach to magic. Applied correctly, your dinner can melt people's brains.

Just like magicians whose secretive guilds monitor the dissemination of tricks, chef's complex procedures are protected and mystified also. Ferran Adrià has often said that he doesn't like explaining the tricks he uses to his customers, because he wants them to be able to react to his food on a purely visceral and emotional level. "You don't want a magician to reveal what's behind his tricks," he says. On the other hand, he is not proprietary about his innovations, and is happy to explain everything to his fellow chefs, one magician to another.

There's a good reason for this. Tricks that are often spectacular become mundane when you know how it's done. David Copperfield flies across the stage, defying gravity and performing aerial somersaults with balletic grace. When you realize he's on a wire it's a downer. If you want to get magical with your food, be careful who you tell.

You also need to be careful about how you many times you present the same dish. Seeing the same flourish twice can be tedious and there's a danger of triviality. Michelin-star chef Santamaria, a traditionalist, branded trick chefs "a gang of charlatans who work to distract snobs... the only truth that matters is the product that comes out of the earth, passes through the ovens to the mouth of the eater, and then is defecated."

Perhaps the answer is to arrange the trickery around the food rather than directly playing with what's on the plate itself. We try to keep the meal itself simple – the setting, dressing and choreography provide the opportunities for sensation. The food must be something guests want to put in their bodies that will leave them satisfied. If fancy techniques or techno-chemicals leave a funny taste in the mouth or your guests need to look for a kebab van to finish the evening, then something is wrong.

Early in 2011 we went on our own food magic adventure. We had become interested in how the restaurants working with a magical sensibility and psychological twists were largely top-end establishments. Enjoying the show costs hundreds of pounds, more than going to see tiger teleporters Siegfried & Roy's Secret Garden in Vegas (As an aside it's worth noting that Siegfried and Roy have published their very own cookbook with recipes from Cher and Eva Longoria). We wanted to put together a kit that would allow anyone to make Michelin-starred food magic and Pancake Day was the key. If you are flipping pancakes in front of people you are already a food showman. With a few tricks, and a bit of flair, you can really impress.

We worked with The Magic Circle to pull together the kit that would allow anyone to create a bio-luminescent sauce using the enzymes that make jellyfish and fireflies glow, brew mathematically correct fractal fluids and make kitchen explosions using chemicals found in any well-stocked cupboard. Some of the ideas developed for the project feature in this book (see pp.36–43).

If you have ever had a magic kit as a child you know they are normally a bit rubbish. We wanted our kit to be the ultimate in culinary spectacle and went all out to get it right. Even down to including a magician's assistant – a leech (see note opposite).

We also learnt a lot too. Magicians Penn and Teller who authored the mischievous *How to Play with your Food* advise taking care in becoming too deeply steeped in the arcane lore of food and magic. If it's all you do, your defining characteristic, you risk becoming the "Novelty Food Guy". No one will talk to you in any other context, about interesting stuff like sex, politics and mermaids. People will want to speak to you but it will be about one thing, make sure it's what you really want.

LEECH HUSBANDRY

Every magician needs an assistant – a lithe and sexy foil to distract the audience at the critical moment of the trick. The best magician's assistants can fit in tiny spaces, come dressed in black and don't answer back! Our magician's assistant was a leech. You can buy them from Biopharm but be sure to get medical grade ones. Not only do they fit the criteria for the ultimate magical helper, they are also the ultimate pet.

You don't need to feed your leech for up to a year. Leeches are super hardy and yours was fed directly before it was sent to you. All you need to do is remember to change the water every couple days or when the leech starts looking sluggish. If you give it a bigger jar you will have to change the water even less. Just remember to have a jar with a tight lid. Otherwise your leech will vanish. They are great escape artists.

Leeches can be fed once a year by going to a good butcher and getting them to fill a sausage skin with fresh blood. Prick the skin with a pin and dangle it in your leech jar. Your assistant will suck on and feed.

We don't recommend proffering your own forearm for a meal but if the leech latches on don't panic and above all don't pull it off. If your leeches are medical grade they are safe. The way to get them off is to wait until they have finished feeding and flop aside or shake a little salt onto them. And, above all, don't share leeches!

Sometime we put our leeches in the finger bowls that people used to cleanse themselves between courses – an unexpected horror that lurks where diners least expect it. This is not always appropriate...

FLOWERS

Tarzan's call echoing across a room packed with jungle fronds and tropical plants sets the tone for a feral meal. Before feasting we head down to a wholesale market and load up on armfuls of the most outrageous plants. In terms of taste we follow the lead of Des Esseintes who believes "stupid and pretentious flowers like the rose... belong in porcelain flowerpots painted by young girls". The decadent (if feeble) hero of *A Rebours* goes for the throat with lurid and exotic hothouse blooms – the more artificial looking the better; we ape his style.

Decorating a table with lush flowers is a relatively recent phenomenon dating from the nineteenth century. Before that, right back into the Middle Ages, the trick was to use the food as the decorative element. For a grand feast dishes would be piled high leaving little room for anything else. Eventually, with Carême's introduction of *service à la Russe* where servants carried successive courses to the table, empty space and wasted opportunity appeared. The gaps on the table were filled with flowers, inedible ornaments and our current obsession, the epergne. If you can track down one of these triffid-like constructs of silver, cut glass and porcelain

and use it for fruit and flowers your table will be ennobled.

As flowers gained in popularity a new and strange language was developed, known as floriography, which gave specific meanings to each species of flora. Some floral symbology remains with us today, with red roses synonymous with amorous love. The ever-anal Victorians, took this to extremes. The gift of a red carnation instead of a rose would mean "Alas for my poor heart!"

Flowers could be used to make or reject otherwise unmentionable propositions. With the right combination of flowers it was possible to say almost anything without the need for words. It was still easy to slip up though – the language was so sophisticated that the sarcastic use of flowers has been documented and evolved quickly so that flower dialects emerged giving different meanings to the same flower. Basil, for example, could symbolize the asking for good wishes but also straightforward hatred.

Today the global flower industry is now worth over a 100 billion dollars a year – no wonder given how expensive cut flowers are. Considering the expense, you'll want to make them work for you.

MESSAGE	FLOWER
Adoration	Dwarf sunflower
Affection	Pear/Morning glory
Agreement	Straw/Lancaster rose
Am I forgotten?	Holly
Be mine	Four-leaf cover
Beauty unknown to possessor	Red daisy
Betrayal	Judas tree/White catchfly
Beware	Oleander
Celibacy	Bachelor's button (Cornflower)
Cold/Cold heartedness	Lettuce
A deadly foe is near	Monkshood
Scandal	Hellebore
Death	Cypress
Hatred	Fumitory
I am worthy of you	White rose
I am dazzled by your charms	Ranunculus
I declare war against you	Tansy/Wild belvedere/Wild liquorice
I engage you for the next dance	Ivy geranium
I have a message for you	Iris
I love you	Red rose
Intoxication	Vine
Naïveté	Silverweed
No/never	Snapdragon
Touch me not	Burdock, Red balsam
You are too bold	Dyplidinia brassinoda

Use floriography to passive aggressively taunt enemies or flirt with suitors when you don't have the courage to speak. The table above should help you with a few basic "phrases" and emotions.

If you aren't in the habit of inviting over enemies for clandestine reproach, but still want to use plenty of flowers, there's still loads you can do. Double up on usage by incorporating edible flowers in the menu. They're both decorative and delicious. Check out the recipe on p.128 to learn the secret. Or set a totally different scene with dangerous and potentially poisonous plant life, evoking a dark sense of adventure and a tingle of excitement. Just don't get the two ideas muddled up.

A huge amount of common household plants are toxic in spite of their often alluring

names. One of our favourites, the Swiss cheese plant (*Monstera deliciosa*) contains calcium oxalate which, when eaten, will cause the mouth and throat to burn and swell, and in high enough doses can be fatal. At the same time, the innocently named Angel's trumpet (owing to it's impressive flowers), is brimming with toxins. These include atropine, hyoscine and hyoscyamine, so eating this plant can be lethal in fairly small quantities. If you're lucky, you get away with moderate pain and terrifying hallucinations. In a recent case, a young man who drank an infusion made from just two of these flowers, spent the afternoon in his grandmother's garden and ended up using shears to amputate his own tongue and penis, under the influence of the poison. This is undoubtedly an afternoon tea *faux pas* and not the kind of behaviour you want from guests. Memorable maybe, but it's always better if they can look back fondly on the meal.

You can of course use flowers for a less risky offensive. Studies have shown that colour can have serious effects on the appetite so use different flowers to encourage or discourage eating. Red and yellow have the greatest effect (as per the success of McDonald's packaging) while blue, a very uncommon colour for non-mouldy food in the natural world, will encourage your guests to eat less – this could always come in handy if your guest has brought extra people without telling you.

One final use for flowers is to decorate the person. Nothing like staging an "urban luau" as suggested by *Playboy*'s food writer Thomas Mario in the 1960s and just draping guests in lush greenery and flowery leys. Flowers from an overgrown garden can, when placed in the hair of a willing female, instantly create a new effects ranging from virgin bride to debauched bacchanalia, depending on how the guests are behaving!

Take care! Too many flowers creates a jungle-like atmosphere but can inhibit cross-table conversation.

EXPLOSIVES AT DINNER

Over the last few years we've collected a bouquet of licences. Some of the licences are straightforward like food hygiene certification and liquor licences. Others are more outlandish like the licence to train performing animals secured for the Rabbit Café, an installation exploring haptic dining with a horde of albino rabbits. Or the chemicals research licence and the pleasure boat licence for the boating lake built on the roof of Selfridges. With application and effort it's possible to secure certification for almost anything from your local authority, including massage parlors and hypnotism.

One of the more unusual licences we possess is to store and sell explosives. Of course explosives are ridiculously dangerous and play no essential part in a meal. Someone losing a limb at your dinner party is always a bummer.

Fires can be a pain too. One of our most harrowing events saw the oven explode in the middle of feeding 300 people during the election all-nighter at The Parliamentary Waffle House - our politically themed eatery. The oven was right there in the middle of the bar so everyone knew something was

'SOMEONE LOSING A LIMB AT YOUR DINNER PARTY IS ALWAYS A BUMMER.'

wrong when it started flaming. Recklessly we carried on serving drinks across the bar while tackling the blaze; probably not the right choice among the election chaos, but people were thirsty. On the plus side the spectacle of the exploding oven united the political factions. Once it was mastered we got a good cheer and it made the night memorable. Now we always try to include explosions and fire.

Set off with style cascading flames and powerful explosive centerpieces make for an epic meal. It's something that people will tell their friends about later.

TABLETOP FIREWORKS

Mentos in coke bottles are for amateurs. You get a fizzy spurt and a puddle to mop up. We like to serve deconstructed fireworks with coffee. Credit goes to inorganic chemist Professor Andrea Sella of UCL who set us off in the right direction.

The raw ingredients are not too hard to dig up with a bit of application. The only chemical we've ever been refused is ammonium nitrate as you have a hard time explaining what you would do with it for a dinner. The idea is to have a safe flame and to change the colour of the flame by adding the various ingredients normally found in fireworks. It's a parlour game that amuses guests as they sit over coffee. Dashing tiny amounts of the special chemicals into the flame makes it dance orange, teal, scarlet and emerald. Done well, this has the conspiratorial thrill of a seance.

For the flame we use methanol, as it burns with a low heat and can be extinguished with water rather than anything exotic. We have to be careful with this stuff, as it's nasty if ingested and highly toxic. As little as 10 ml can cause permanent blindness by destroying the optic nerve and 30 ml is potentially fatal. Sam once swallowed some by accident but made it through – happily there are a couple of antidotes readily available in every kitchen. Sodium bicarbonate helps with metabolic acidosis, and ethanol (in every alcoholic beverage) is the foremost antidote through competitive inhibition (meaning you urinate it out rather than it dissolving your optic nerve). So, don't swallow any methanol or you will have to drink a lot of spirits.

For legal reasons, we don't advise you try this at home!

SOMETHING BIGGER

If you have more people to impress reach for something more substantial. We pop along to our local theatrical special effects shop, Stage Electrics, and raid their shelves for pyrotechnics and explosion effects.

One of the best and easiest to use is the confetti cannon. They are cheap and awesome for creating a sense of spectacle, and you can even fill them with edibles to rain down on the crowd (encourage them to turn their mouths to the sky). Use the cannon to punctuate an important moment - wedding vows, someone jumping out of a super-sized cake, the best bit of a concert.

Follow the instructions from the hire shop depending on the equipment they use. Fill with confetti, glitter or edible wafers. While at the shop take the chance to pick up blood capsules, spray on cobwebs and smoke in a can.

WEDDING EXPLOSIONS

In the end we got so carried away by explosives that we launched a food explosion service for weddings. One of our technicians lays charges within the wedding cake (or food of choice), which is detonated at the climax of the evening. To celebrate the launch of the service, we collaborated with photographer Ryan Hopkinson on spectacular photographs exploring what happens when powerful explosives are detonated inside jellies. The explosions were documented by Ryan, using a camera shooting at the super high speed of 240 frames per second in 2,000 pixel resolution, allowing the disintegration of the jelly to be studied in fascinating detail (see overleaf).

On making a booking with us, a trained explosives technician (member of the Association of Stage Pyrotechnicians) liaises with the wedding cake provider on setting the charges and arranging risk assessments and method statements with the venue so they aren't too alarmed. They attend on the day of the wedding to set the explosives, rig the detonator and supervise the explosion. All explosives are transported within containers meeting the Ministry of Defence (MOD)'s SEAP 4 security standards as referred to in JSP440.

Wedding cakes can be brutally stodgy. Blowing the cake up spares the stomach after a heavy meal and is a good way to wake guests up for the speeches!

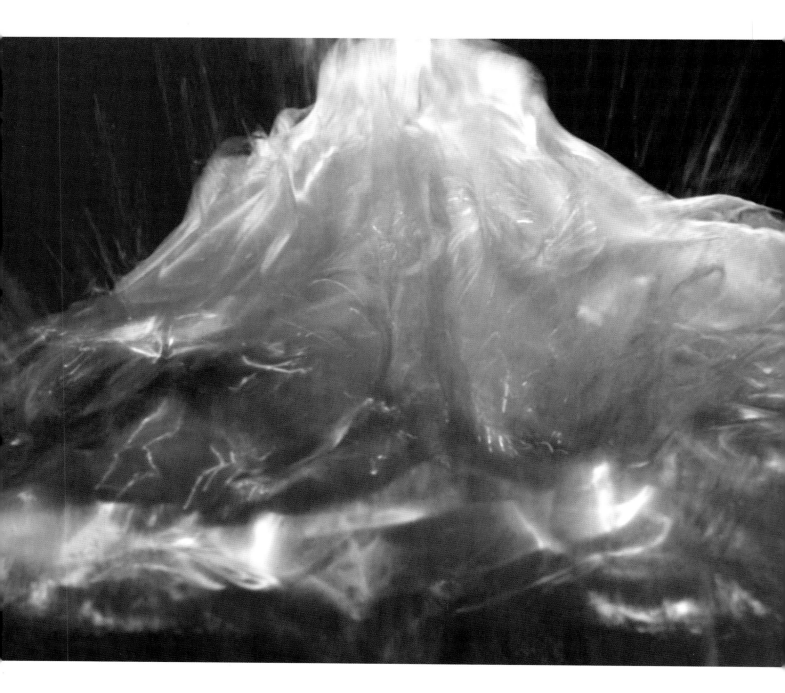

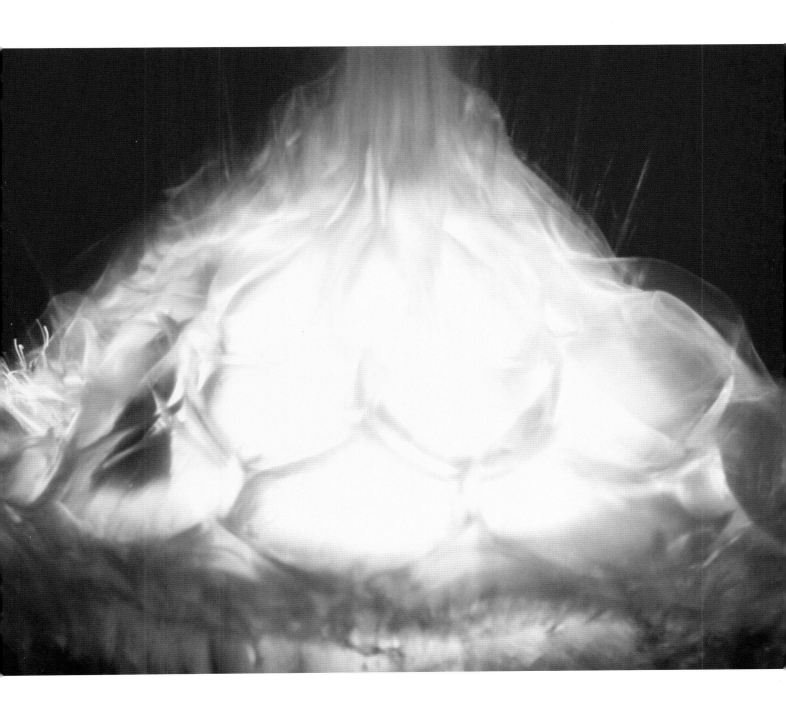

SERVICE & UNIFORMS

Everyone knows, when being served any meal, that the waiting staff have the power to make or marr the whole experience. You forgive a restaurant a lot if the service is good, while a rude waiter can turn the food to ashes in your mouth. Worse still, everyone knows that serving staff have the power to spit in your food, so the ideal waiter is one whose deportment and demeanor tells you that the immense pride they take in their work makes it unlikely they'll take any such liberties.

Uniform plays a huge roll in this, as it will be seen and judged long before anyone's had a chance to overwhelm the guests with their politeness. Serving staff are the kitchen's ambassadors and, as such, their costume must be a testament to the quality of the coming meal, as well as the ethos of the whole restaurant/company.

Some bizarre research seems to suggest that the appearance of service staff has a marked effect on diners. Professor Michael Lynn of the Cornell University School of Hotel Administration recently correlated the relationship between size of tips left for waitresses and their physical attributes. Unfairly perhaps, the survey found that waitresses with bigger breasts were a lot more successful, as were the slimmer and blonder types. While customers claimed they were rewarding service, it was found that quality of service actually had a smaller than 2 per cent effect on the tip given.

It is very hard to tie Bompas & Parr down to one uniform in particular, given the ever-changing nature of our work. Costume designers have been given commissions as esoteric as "Crystal Maze Series One meets Kubrick on a mountain" and our servers have ended up in an eclectic range of outfits, such as the purple "chocolate waterfall hats" and on occasion – notably the naked man in the popcorn dispenser of our Scratch 'n' Sniff Cinema very little at all.

In every case, however, our inspiration for clothing starts with the mythical figure of "the continental waiter". The idea of a proud career in the service industry is not particularly prevalent in Britain where it tends to be nothing more than a stopgap. For the (ideal) continental waiter, table service is an art and the uniform needs to be clean and neat and practical. It won't trail through soup as they squeeze between tables or restrict them as the wine is poured. In general, when green espadrilles and whips are not being handed out, we provide bow ties and carvers' jackets (these can purchased from Denny's Uniforms, see Suppliers), which fulfil all the important criteria. A crisp, plain white shirt and jacket is evidence of the clean environment behind the scenes, simple enough to blend into the background so

that the staff aren't a distraction, but noticeable enough that they can be located when needed.

For some of our events, the staff are more akin to seers and sorcerers, revealing the food and the stories behind it. Here, showmanship is as important as the outfit and it is often a good idea to hire the histrionic. As many waiting staff in the UK are actors between jobs, this can be a real boon for companies like ours. In any case, servers must be the authority on the food and therefore they must be believable. Uniforms of any kind instantly give authority to the bearer so choose some clean (and preferably busty) actors and dress them accordingly.

Page 47: The uniform from *The Voyage of Discovery*. Our designer, Tour de Force, created what committed explorers would wear to visit a lush tropical Riviera for cocktails.
Left: Servers biting into the main dish is rarely appropriate.
Right: Waitresses at our *Black Banquet*.

PLANNING

This isn't famously the most fun aspect of a party but it is wholly necessary and you'll thank yourself later for every minute you put in before the feast, when your guests are raising bumper cups oveflowing with mead to you by the end.

For a simple project, planning can be quick and easy and seems less important. It's when your task involves getting 2000 people to enjoy a boat trip on the roof of Selfridges over one (speedily approaching) weekend that you realize the merit of proper planning.

When we first started off and weren't as confident as we are today, we applied ultra-planning to our first feast, a Victorian Breakfast at Warwick Castle. It was for an overwhelming and luxurious 12-course breakfast (clocking in at over 4,000 calories per person). We went for planning overkill as Harry drew up full architectural plans for each course explaining the table laying and re-laying (given the thousands of pieces of cutlery required, the table had to be re-laid three times), food production flows and serving choreography.

In the end, we were of course glad we had done all this. It meant that the whisky-laced porridge, and the rest of the mega meal arrived on time and the waiting staff knew where they had to be for the most part. If the staff had had enough time to start sampling the food themselves we may have been in trouble, given the alcoholic content of the breakfast, which incorporated champagne, Bordeaux, Burgundy, whisky and crème de menthe.

When it comes to planning we look to the lessons learnt by the scientists entering Biosphere 2, the huge, yet totally cut off, dome complex built in Oracle, Arizona, US. It was set up to research ecosystems and the possibility of creating something Earth-like on foreign planets. Given that they were going to be locked in for two years, the scientists had to be pretty prepared. Though the well-planned diet left them hungry for the entire first year (they only had 1,700 calories apiece per day), they showed that their survival was just about possible without the need for anything from the outside world. Several of the other species they brought in were not so lucky, being slaughtered for meat to supplement the meagre rations.

Plan how to make everything go perfectly but at the same time prepare for the chance that it might not. Happily then, we always work hard on the risk assessment with the result that the Bompas & Parr accident book is almost entirely lacking in entries. There is, of course, "Tasha: blister on palm of hand due to repeated stripping motion." Some things are just impossible to prepare for...

It all sounds obvious, but if you remember these few things you will be fine. Get organized and divide up the roles. Take the helm on food and then delegate the sound systems, drinks and surprises. If you are planning a proper feast (we'd hope you are) you wouldn't be able to do it all by yourself anyway, and don't forget the unbeatable power of a simple list.

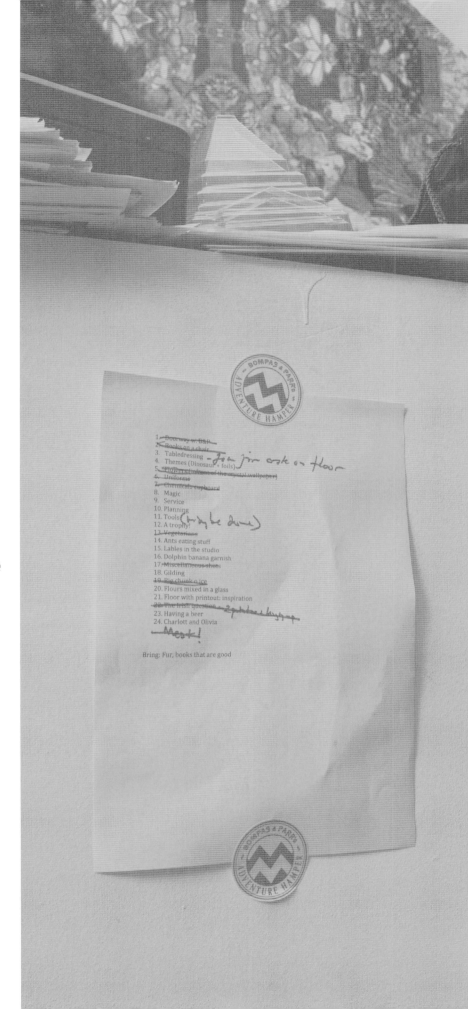

RECIPES

CANAPÉS

QUAIL'S EGGS WITH CHILLI & 24 CARAT GOLD

Not so much a "recipe", but quail's eggs look the part and the peeling will give your guests something to do while they are hanging out waiting for the main event to kick off. Splashing out on some edible gold (E-number 175 – the European code for gold as a food additive) always creates a talking point.

SERVES 8

48 quail's eggs
10 g/¼ oz chilli powder
30 g/1 oz table salt
6 sheets of edible gold leaf

Bring a large pan of water to the boil. Have a bowl filled with iced water ready. Boil the eggs for 2½ minutes, then remove with a slotted spoon and place them straight into the chilled water. Remove the cooled eggs from the water and dry with kitchen paper (paper towels). Keep the eggs refrigerated.

For the dip, start by combining the chilli powder with the salt in a large bowl. Using the tines of a fork, add the sheets of the gold leaf and use the fork to "whisk" the gold into the salt mix. The idea is to break up the gold so that you end up with evenly distributed gold among the red powder.

One hour before serving, remove the eggs from the refrigerator and arrange en pyramide in a silver dish. Invite your guests to peel their own eggs before dipping in the chilli, gold and salt. Have a bowl on hand for the discarded shells.

SPICED ROAST ALMONDS

These are a really posh version of honey-roasted peanuts. For added authenticity why not hide a picture of a semi-naked girl under the pile of nuts like you get behind packs of pub peanuts (Double-D nuts!)? Watch yourself with the bowl of them. They are dangerously compelling and you could end up ploughing through the lot before your guests arrive.

SERVES 8

300 g/10½ oz/2 cups almonds
2 tbsp honey
2 tbsp water
2 tsp groundnut oil
25 g/1 oz/2 tbsp caster (superfine) sugar
½ tsp salt
½ tsp ground cinnamon
1 tsp hot paprika

Preheat the oven to 180°C/ 350°F/ Gas Mark 4.

Spread the almonds out on a baking sheet and roast in the oven for about 10 minutes, until beginning to colour.

Combine the honey, water and oil together in a pan and, when bubbling, add the hot nuts. Cook over a moderate heat until the nuts are thoroughly coated and the syrup has evaporated. Remove from the heat.

Mix together the sugar and spices and tip into the pan. Stir thoroughly so that the nuts are coated. Tip the nuts back onto the baking sheet, spread out and leave to cool.

CHEESE STRAWS

This is an excellent way to use up the leftover puff pastry from making a vol-au-vent. If you've gone to all the effort to make the pastry it is comforting to know that you can put it to good use. Unlike most pastry, if you just push the trimmings from your vol-au-vent into a ball you won't get a fine result when you make it into something else. This is because all the many layers get jumbled up and it won't rise properly – a real waste when you can use the handy technique detailed below.

MAKES 40

½ quantity of puff pastry
(see vol-au-vent pastry recipe
on pp.211–3)
plain flour, for dusting
250 g/9 oz Parmesan cheese
1 egg beaten with 1 tsp water

Preheat the oven to 180°C/350°F/Gas Mark 4.

Cut all the trimmings of pastry down so that they are long thin rectangles. You will be left with some little triangular pieces too. Hang onto these. On a floured work surface, use a little water to join the pastry together, butting up each piece to one another and pushing lightly on the joints with your fingers to hold them together. Grate a quarter of the cheese over one half of the pastry. Push in slightly with a floured rolling pin. Now fold the pastry in half. You may lose bits of the pastry but just patch it back together as best you can. Roll the pastry back out to its original size and repeat the cheese and folding operation another two times. By now the pastry and cheese should be fairly well combined.

Cut the pastry into 4 portions and roll out each section until it is 3 mm/⅛ in thick. Trim the edges to form a neat rectangle and brush with the beaten egg. Sprinkle over a quarter of the remaining cheese. Cut into strips about 2 cm/¾ in wide and twist each strip a few times before arranging on a silicone baking mat. Continue until the sheet is used up then do the same for the remaining sheets.

Bake in the oven for about 12 minutes, or until the pastry is cooked through. You may need to cook the twists in batches. Once cooled, these will keep for a few weeks in an airtight container. The blocks of pastry can be frozen for use another time.

SURREALIST STUFFED EGGS

– DEVILLED EGGS ARE A BIT NAFF BUT THEY ARE A CLASSIC AND LOOK PRETTY TOO –

Surrealist stuffed eggs take the preparation to a new dimension. This simple canapé is based on the surrealist game Exquisite Corpse – the one where you fold a piece of paper into three and everyone draws one bit of the body before passing it onto their neighbour. The results are always embarrassing and reveal far more information than you need to know about the people sitting next to you.

The recipe is based on classic devilled eggs but this time there are three fillings and three toppings all swapped about to create all manner of flavour combinations. We first gave it a go for the opening banquet for the Barbican Art Gallery's Surreal House Exhibition. It was a night of Buster Keaton movies set to smell, waitresses in hopelessly impractical deep sea divers outfits for the final course (lobsters and monsters) and the soundtrack for the banquet generated by an operational egg synthesizer. Fun aside, the surrealists took food seriously, realizing its strength to provoke and engage audiences. It was a handy tool to arouse interest and emotion.

Dalí particularly took an interest pushing it far beyond the acceptable bounds of the table. As he puts it himself, "At the age of six I wanted to be a cook. At seven I wanted to be Napoleon. And my ambition has been growing steadily ever since."

MAKES 36 CANAPÉS
18 hen's eggs
25 g/1 oz mayonnaise mixed with 1 tsp mustard and 3 hard-boiled yolks (see method)
50 ml/1¾ fl oz/scant ¼ cup whipped double (heavy) cream mixed with 1 tsp icing (confectioners') sugar
50 g/1¾ oz/scant ¼ cup goat's curd mixed with 1 tsp double cream
12 mini asparagus tips, blanched
12 anchovies
12 small pieces of chorizo

Boil the eggs for 9 minutes and drop into a large bowl of cold water. You may need to boil up in batches. Once cool, peel the eggs, slice in half and remove the yolks with a teaspoon, saving 3 for the mayonnaise mixture.

Fill one-third of the eggs with the mayonnaise mixture, the next third with the cream and the remainder with the goat's curd. Similarly top each egg with the asparagus, anchovies and chorizo so that each filling has its fair share of toppings. Serve on a large platter arranged in straight lines or patterns.

CHICKEN LOLLIPOPS

These cute little drumsticks are the stuff of carnivore's dreams: a clean bone to hang onto and a nugget of juicy meat to bite into. The technique for making the lollipops can be found on pp.214-5.

Prepare as many lollipops as you need. Keep refrigerated until you want to cook them. They can be prepared in advance and frozen. Below are three different ways to cook the lollipops, which one you choose depends on how much time you have and what the theme of your feast is.

MAKES ABOUT 20
CHICKEN LOLLIPOPS
1 kg/2 lb 4 oz chicken thighs

FOR SOUTHERN-FRIED LOLLIPOPS
50 g/1³/₄ oz/generous ¹/₃ cup plain
(all purpose) flour
1 tsp salt
1 tsp cayenne pepper
1 tsp chilli powder
groundnut oil, for frying

FOR STICKY TERIYAKI/
MARMALADE LOLLIPOPS
see p.94 or p.96

FOR CRISPY COATED LOLLIPOPS
2 eggs, beaten
50 g/1³/₄ oz/generous ¹/₃ cup plain
(all purpose) flour
salt and black pepper
100 g/3¹/₂ oz/¹/₃ cup panko
breadcrumbs
groundnut oil, for frying
aïoli, to serve

For Southern-fried lollipops

In a large bowl, mix all of the dry ingredients together. Add the chicken thighs and mix with your hands until they are coated. Dust off the excess flour and shallow-fry on a low heat until crispy and cooked through, about 15 minutes. Remove with a slotted spoon and remove any excess oil with kitchen paper (paper towels). Serve while still hot and crispy. They can be kept warm in a low oven for an hour if necessary.

For sticky teriyaki lollipops/sticky marmalade lollipops

Use the tropical chicken sauce recipe on p.94 or the marinade for the marmalade quail recipe (see p.96) and cook the lollipops in a hot oven for about 25 minutes, or until the sauce has gone suitably sticky and the chicken is brown.

For crispy coated lollipops

Beat the eggs together and slowly incorporate the flour. Season with salt and pepper. Have the breadcrumbs ready in a shallow dish. Dip the meat of the lollipop only into the egg and then roll in the breadcrumbs. Repeat a second time.

Shallow-fry at about 160°C/325°F until they are crispy and cooked through, about 10 minutes. Serve with aïoli (or for a cheat's version mix 1 crushed garlic glove into 250 g/9 oz/generous 1 cup mayonnaise).

PASTEL SANDWICHES

The impressive thing about pastel sandwiches is the bread. It suggests that you've either bothered to charm a baker in to baking it for you or are a talented baker yourself. Luckily you don't need to be skilled at either for these to impress. What you need for these "crusts off" sandwiches is plastic white bread – exactly what you get when you bake it yourself using packet bread mix. The advantage of the packet mix is that it has plenty of additives so it won't go stale too quickly, it also slices really well and is foolproof.

MAKES 60 SMALL SANDWICHES
3 x 500 g/1 lb 2 oz packets
of white bread mix
red, green and yellow food dye

FOR THE FILLINGS
6-cm/2$\frac{1}{2}$-in section cucumber
50 g/1$\frac{3}{4}$ oz/scant $\frac{1}{4}$ cup goat's curd
75 g/2$\frac{3}{4}$ oz smoked salmon
1 tsp grated horseradish
1 tsp crème fraîche
4 hen's eggs
25 g/1 oz/1$\frac{1}{2}$ tbsp mayonnaise
20 saffron threads
salt and black pepper

Preheat the oven to 180°C/350°F/Gas Mark 4.

Start by baking the bread. You will need three 450 g/1 lb loaf tins (pans) and you can do all three at once if you have enough tins. If not, space out over a day or so. Follow the instructions on the packet but add some dye to the warm water to create the desired colour. You will need a fair amount of dye to create an even pastel colour. Even once you've added the coloured water to the bread there is still opportunity to add more dye if you think it needs it – it will mix in.

While the bread is baking get to work on the fillings. We like to use fillings that are "spreadable" as they look best. Here are some suggestions – it's not hard to improvise others.

Goat's curd and cucumber filling
Peel the cucumber, slice in half lengthways and remove the seeds with a teaspoon. Cut into a fine dice and mix with the goat's curd.

Smoked salmon and horseradish
Cut the smoked salmon into fine dice (about 2 mm/$\frac{1}{16}$ in) and mix in the horseradish and crème fraîche.

Saffron egg mayonnaise
Hard-boil the eggs, peel and cool. Beat the eggs in a kitchen mixer until the eggs have broken up. Mix in the mayonnaise and the saffron, then season.

To assemble the sandwiches
Slice the bread into thin slices then layer up sandwiches as follows:
pink bread – cucumber filling – green bread – cucumber filling – pink bread
yellow bread – salmon filling – pink bread – salmon filling – yellow bread
green bread – egg filling – yellow bread – egg filling – green bread
Slice off the crusts and cut each sandwich into three rectangular pieces. A card template, about 3 x 6 cm (1 x 2 in) is a useful tool.

SNAILS EN ATTELET

A tabletop snail hunt can be a thrilling if gruesome way to start a meal. Arm your guests with skewers, place a mini terrarium filled with the live snails on the table and allow the guests to pick (and hunt) their own. If the skewers can be identified in some way (like a little flag) then you can present your guests with their now cooked snail several courses later in the meal.

Our fascination with snails and live action hunts started when Harry designed and fabricated our very own solid silver *attelets* or "meat jewellery". *Atellets*, effectively elaborate skewers or posh kebab sticks, represent a forgotten piece of kitchenalia once used to truss quail and garnish pigs' heads. Chefs threaded whole truffles, snails and blanched coxcombs onto grand feasting dishes such as a boar's head. Georgian "celebrity" chef Antonin Carême who cooked for George IV, Napoleon and Tsar Alexander I, championed the use of a great number of *attelets* with his dishes, but sadly in the last 200 years, these elegant ornaments fell out of favour. You can pick up original *attelets* in antique markets mistakenly being flogged as hatpins or letter openers – their use is far more noble.

Harry used 3D computer modelling, rapid prototyping and traditional silver-smithing techniques to make our very own interpretation. By a strange twist of fate they were first used as the jewellery for designer Adam Entwisle's fashion show. It was pretty weird sitting in the front seeing our cooking equipment paraded down the catwalk. Models wore them as pendants and necklaces, and in their hair and piercings. Here's what the designer said: "The desire! Is it the food or the beauty? Or is it both?"

After this we thought it would be best to buckle down and find a proper food application. Snails held the key. The hunt and subsequent presentation of snails *en attelet* (threaded into another dish) provides table magic. It's worth bearing in mind that if there are vegetarians present you probably won't get away with serving this dish. There will be a ruckus.

See overleaf for recipe.

SERVES 16

32 prepared snails (see method)
16 live snails (see method)
1 tbsp butter
2 garlic cloves, minced
2 tsp finely chopped parsley

Make a terrarium for the live snails. We used a cake stand with a glass dome. People are endlessly fascinated by them.

The trick to turning this round quickly is to buy both live snails and prepped and blanched snails ready for eating. Send the live snails out in the terrarium at the start of the meal. Post-hunt, swap them out for your cooked snails (taking note of the distinctive skewers so everyone gets what they imagine to be the snail they caught).

The snails for eating are ready prepared and blanched, then it's just a case of reheating them in some butter and minced garlic.

Sprinkle with parsley before serving and serve while still hot, perhaps stuck into an epic meat dish.

A note on the attelets: Cocktail swords or customized barbecue skewers would be appropriate too. If you use real atteletts you have to be pretty careful when serving a dish garnished with them, otherwise they are all pocketed! Harry recommends counting them back in as the dishes are cleared.

FROG'S LEGS

Frog's legs are another fun canapé that doesn't require too much skill in the kitchen – just sensible shopping. We buy packs of frogs legs ready cooked and frozen to make this peasant-style dish. They are best dusted in flour mixed with lemon zest and then pan-fried in butter until crispy. The end results are feral and you can well understand how 3.2 billion frogs are eaten every year around the world.

SERVES 8

500 g/1 lb 2 oz prepared frozen frog's legs

100 g/3¹/₂ oz/scant ³/₄ cup plain (all purpose) flour

grated zest of 2 lemons

salt and black pepper

50 g/1³/₄ oz/3¹/₂ tbsp butter

25 ml/1 fl oz/2 tbsp olive oil

4 garlic cloves, crushed

Defrost the frog's legs. Mix together the flour and lemon zest and season liberally with salt and pepper. Dry the frog's legs on kitchen paper (paper towels) and then dust in the flour mix.

Melt the butter and oil in a large frying pan. When sizzling, add the frog's legs and cook over a moderate heat until the legs are crispy, about 5 minutes. Near the end of the cooking, add the garlic to flavour the legs slightly.

Serve immediately, with homemade mayonnaise (see p.208) for dipping.

SMOKED EEL, CELERIAC REMOULADE AND OATCAKE

Eels - part snake, part fish, they have bemused scientist for hundreds of years. They spawn in the western Atlantic, head over to Europe, swim up rivers, slither over wet ground if necessary and somehow get all the way back to the Sargasso Sea again. No wonder they are endangered. It might be politically incorrect, but it's worth trying eel while you can still get them, as they are delicious.

Smoked eel can be bought online from many specialist suppliers. If you are up for an adventure getting up early and heading over to London's Billingsgate market to visit "Mick the eel man" is well worth it. He keeps his live eels in perforated metal drawers that have a torrent of water flowing through to keep them in peak condition until they are dispatched. Stop for a bacon, scallop and Cheddar butty from the café when you are done shopping.

SERVES 8

100 g/3½ oz smoked eel fillets
¼ quantity celeriac remoulade
(see p.208)
32 mini oatcakes
1 tsp finely chopped tarragon

Slice the eel and put to one side. Put a teaspoonful of the remoulade onto each oatcake and top with the slices of eel. Garnish with the chopped tarragon. So simple.

SOUPS & STARTERS

STEAK TARTARE

Like steak Diane and banana flambé, steak tartare used to require a table show. The maître d' would not only stir in the flavourings to individual requirements but come to the table armed with a sharpened blade to chop the meat too. The advantage of this dish is that you can roll with it in many different ways. We often do it as a canapé but it also works well as a dish for people to make by themselves at the table.

The easiest and most fun thing to do is to just drop everything on the table and invite your guests to satisfy themselves. In every group there is invariably someone who likes playing with sharp knives. As with anything served raw, make sure you buy a decent piece of meat from a reputable butcher. Always keep it well chilled and be scrupulous about your kitchen and personal hygiene.

SERVES 8 AS A STARTER

8 eggs
1 kg/2 lb 4 oz fillet, sirloin or rump (round) steak
2 tbsp finely diced cornichons
2 tbsp mustard
2 tbsp finely diced shallots
2 tbsp finely chopped parsley
salt and black pepper
Worcestershire sauce
Tabasco sauce

Crack open the eggs, trying to split each shell neatly in half. Divide the yolks from the whites and place an egg yolk in one of the half shells. Use the egg box to keep them upright. Save the whites for meringues or give them to someone on a faddy diet.

Place the steak on a roomy wooden chopping board. Place the cornichons, mustard, shallots and parsley in separate small dishes and have the other ingredients to hand.

To serve

Carefully slice the steak into small cubes, about 3 x 3 mm/$\frac{1}{6}$ x $\frac{1}{6}$ in and place in a bowl. A razor sharp knife is essential. The chopped meat must be eaten immediately. It is possible to prepare a couple of hours in advance but the meat should be kept in the bowl over ice so that it does not become mushy. Invite your guests to help themselves to the assemblage of ingredients and mix to their own tastes with the egg yolk to bind it together. Grilled slices of sourdough are an ideal accompaniment. If you are lucky enough to live next to a McDonald's, run over for a few large portions of fries.

POTTED CRAB

This is an easy starter to prepare ahead. It can be scaled up to feed hundreds without difficulty and takes seconds to serve. If you don't have enough ramekins you could make a terrine in a loaf tin (pan). You will need to unmould and slice it to serve - a hot towel held around the tin should be enough to melt a little of the butter and get it sliding out. If you plan to slice it then this should be done while the potted crab is still chilled. Before you begin it's worth forking through the crabmeat to look for stray pieces of shell, there's nothing more annoying than chomping down on a bit unexpectedly.

SERVES 8 AS A STARTER

1 large shallot (about 50 g/1³/₄ oz), finely diced
250 g/9 oz/1¹/₈ cups butter, plus
50 g/1³/₄ oz/3¹/₂ tbsp butter, to seal
25 ml/1 fl oz/1 tbsp sherry
1 tsp cayenne pepper
¹/₄ whole nutmeg, freshly grated
200 g/7 oz white crabmeat
200 g/7 oz brown crabmeat
juice of ¹/₂ lemon
salt and black pepper
rye bread, toasted, to serve

Cook the shallot gently in about 20 g/ ³/₄ oz/1¹/₂ tbsp of the butter in a small pan for a few minutes until the shallot has turned translucent. Add the sherry and spices and continue cooking for a few more minutes, stirring frequently. Add the remaining butter to the pan and continue to cook for about 5 minutes, or until all the butter has melted. Remove the pan from the heat and pass the buttery onion mix through a sieve (strainer), making sure to squeeze as much liquid as possible from the shallots.

Set a metal bowl over a large bowl filled with ice and pour in the butter. Whisk gently to create a thick creamy consistency then add the crabmeat, lemon juice, salt and pepper. Portion into 8 ramekins and refrigerate until the butter is set. Melt the remaining butter and pour over the top of the potted crab to seal completely. Refrigerate until set.

This can be made a day ahead. Be sure to remove from the refrigerator at least 1 hour before serving to let the butter soften. Serve with toasted rye bread.

POTTED MUSHROOMS

SERVES 8

FOR THE CUMBERLAND JELLY

rind and juice of 1 lemon
rind and juice of 1 orange
100 ml/3^1/$_2$ fl oz/generous ^{1}/$_3$ cup port
1 tsp mustard powder
1 tsp ground ginger
100 g/3^1/$_2$ oz redcurrant jelly
3 leaves of gelatine

FOR THE POTTED MUSHROOMS

1 packet (30 g/1 oz) dried porcini mushrooms
1 large shallot (about 50 g/1^3/$_4$ oz), finely diced
250 g/9 oz/1^1/$_8$ cups butter, plus 50 g/1^3/$_4$ oz/3^1/$_2$ tbsp butter, to seal
600 g/1 lb 5 oz mixed mushrooms (eg. button, field, etc.), chopped into 10-mm/^{1}/$_2$-in dice
1 tsp cayenne pepper
^{1}/$_4$ whole nutmeg, freshly grated
25 ml/1 fl oz/1 tbsp sherry
juice of ^{1}/$_2$ lemon

A tasty vegetarian version of potted crab is potted mushrooms. Uncharacteristically, we prefer this to the crab version (p.75). The process is very similar. For added show we like to set a layer of Cumberland jelly in the bottom of the mould. It does wonders to improve the brown slab of the mushrooms, although of course it also sneakily adds meat to the dish!

Start by making the jelly. Or, if you are true to your cause, skip it altogether. Add the rinds, juices, port and spices to a small saucepan. Heat gently for about 15 minutes to let the flavours of the rind transfer. Stir in the redcurrant jelly and strain the mixture through a fine sieve. You should obtain about 300 ml/10^1/$_2$ fl oz/1^1/$_4$ cups of liquid. If not add a splash more port to make it up to that amount. If you have too much liquid, remove a bit. This is important, to make the jelly set.

Chop up the leaves of gelatine and soak in a small saucepan for a few minutes in 100 ml/3^1/$_2$ fl oz/generous ^{1}/$_3$ cup of the liquid. Put the pan onto the lowest heat and stir constantly and briskly until the gelatine is melted. Remove from the heat and add the rest of the liquid giving it a good stir. Pour the jelly into the bottom of the moulds that you are using (either 8 individual ramekins or a loaf tin). Use your intuition to decide how deep to pour. Don't make it too thin or unmoulding will be tricky. Place in the refrigerator to set.

For the mushrooms, start by soaking the porcini mushrooms in 100 ml/3^1/$_2$ fl oz/generous ^{1}/$_3$ cup boiling water.

In a small pan, cook the shallot in 20 g/^{3}/$_4$ oz/1^1/$_2$ tbsp of the butter (from the 250 g/9 oz/1^1/$_8$ cups) and, when soft, add the diced mixed mushrooms and spices and cook until reduced in volume by two-thirds. Add the sherry to deglaze the pan, then add the porcini mushrooms and soaking water. Boil until there is about a tablespoon of liquid left. Add the lemon juice and the remaining 230 g/8^1/$_2$ oz/generous 1 cup butter and heat gently until the butter has melted.

Whisk the mixture over an ice bath as with the crab (see p.75) and divide among the ramekins or loaf tin, being careful not too disturb the jelly too much. Refrigerate.

When the mushrooms are set, melt the 50g/1^3/$_4$ oz/3^1/$_2$ tbsp butter and pour over the mushrooms. Return to the refrigerator for a final set.

MOCK TURTLE SOUP WITH PERFUMED QUAIL'S EGGS

SERVES 8

2 tbsp olive oil

300 g/10½ oz/scant 2 cups onion, diced

2 litres/3½ pints/8 cups vegetable stock (see below)

300 g/10½ oz/2 cups potato, diced

225 g/8 oz watercress

225 g/8 oz spinach

sea salt and black pepper

8 perfumed quail's eggs (see below)

2 tsp basil seeds

FOR THE VEGETABLE STOCK

2 litres/3½ pints/8 cups water

2 onions, roughly chopped

2 carrots, peeled and roughly chopped

2 celery sticks, roughly chopped

pinch of sea salt

8 black peppercorns, crushed

1 bay leaf

FOR THE PERFUMED QUAIL'S EGGS

12 quail's eggs

yellow food dye

big pinch of saffron threads

Traditional mock turtle soup is made by boiling the head of a calf and was a popular Victorian dish. Calves' heads are tricky to procure these days: strangely it's much easier to boil a turtle, especially if you live in America. We developed this supermarket-friendly and politically correct mock turtle for *Dining with Alice*, an all-out theatrical dining adventure held at Elsing Hall, Norfolk. We had to find a starter that was easy to serve, tasted good cold, was vegetarian and was a bit weird, but not too weird so that everyone would eat it. Over 2,000 people tucked in, so chances are it won't offend anyone.

This recipe only qualifies as "turtlesque" because it of its vivid colour. The real intrigue lies in the perfumed quail's egg lurking at the bottom of the soup.

The inclusion of basil seeds adds a satisfying slimy crunch to the mix. By soaking the seeds in water for a few minutes they soften, expand and end up looking like frogspawn. We buy basil seeds at the garden centre, and Asian shops stock them too.

Put all the ingredients for the vegetable stock in a saucepan. Bring to the boil and cook for 20 minutes. Leave to cool. If you have herbs to hand (thyme, parsley, etc.) add a few sprigs after the stock has come off the heat.

For the quail's eggs, bring a small pan of water to the boil and cook the eggs for 3 minutes so that they are hard-boiled. Drain and cool in a bowl of iced water. Peel the eggs then place them in small bowl or jar, top up with water and add a good few drops of yellow food dye and the big pinch of saffron. Allow the eggs to infuse and colour for as much time as you have (up to a few days).

For the soup, add the oil to a saucepan and sweat off the onion being careful not to brown them. Add the vegetable stock, bring to a simmer and add the diced potato. When the potato is cooked (it will crumble under the point of a knife) take the pan off the heat, add the watercress and spinach and stir until the leaves are wilted. Blend the soup using a stick blender or liquidizer until smooth. Season the soup, bearing in mind that it will be served chilled, so add slightly more salt to compensate for the cold. Refrigerate until chilled.

To assemble the soup, soak the basil seeds in a bowl of water for a couple of minutes so that they expand. Place a perfumed quail's egg in the bottom of each bowl, ladle over the soup and sprinkle on a few drained basil seeds.

SEA URCHIN OEUFS BROUILLÉS

Sea urchins guarantee a "wow" from guests. They are a little hard to find but this is an easy recipe that makes a smart amuse-bouche. To make this properly you need to be adept at cooking eggs. Scrambled eggs are always made badly. Once you have the technique down it's easy to transform eggs, butter and salt into a dish of destiny. See p.210 for the technique. When you get really good call them *oeufs brouillés* – it sounds better.

Sam spent four years on an egg-based diet and so he now proclaims that he can boil the best egg ever. Even legendary French chef Jacques Pépin says you can't improve a boiled egg so maybe Sam's claim is true (along with everyone else). Even if you can't cook you should at least be able to say that you cook something better than anyone else. It's a British tradition. Master scrambling eggs and someone might even believe you.

Fresh urchins can be hard to track down but decent fishmongers should be able to get them. In season (October–April) they can be readily bought at Billingsgate Market, London, where they fly them over from France. They freeze well too, but it's best to do this after you have prepped them.

SERVES 8

8 sea urchins
8 eggs
75 g/2³/₄ oz/6 tbsp unsalted butter
1 tsp finely chopped parsley,
to garnish

To open the urchins, use a pair of sharp scissors and a folded tea (dish) towel to cut a circle out of the concave side. Discard the top, then scoop out the contents with a small teaspoon saving the flesh and roe. The sacks of "flesh" are actually the sexual organs of the animal, but that is not necessarily a detail you want to share. Wash the shells and set aside. Keep everything refrigerated until ready to use.

When ready to serve, warm the shells in a low oven. This not only provides heat retention, but sterilizes the shells. Make scrambled eggs using 8 eggs, as described on p.210. When the eggs are "relaxing", add the urchin flesh and roe and continue cooking until done. Carefully check seasoning – eggs can't take a lot of salt and the urchin is relatively salty, so you may not need to add more.

Spoon the eggs into the shells and garnish with finely chopped parsley. Serve at once.

BUSH OF CRAYFISH IN VIKING HERBS

AN IMPRESSIVE CATCH
SERVES 16 AS A STARTER
5 kg/11 lb crayfish

FOR THE *FUMET*
1 bottle of white wine
3 onions, chopped
4 celery sticks, chopped
10 peppercorns
1 star anise
1 head garlic, cut in half
1 tbsp sea salt
3 litres/5 pints/3¼ quarts water
½ bunch of lemon thyme
1 bunch of dill (Viking herbs)

FOR THE *FUMET* REDUCTION
1 tbsp olive oil
1 onion, chopped
2 celery sticks, chopped
1 glass of Cognac
3 tomatoes, skinned, deseeded and
chopped (keep skins and seeds)
250 ml/9 fl oz/generous 1 cup Noilly
Prat

TO FINISH
1 tower (see overleaf)
bunches of dill, parsley, etc.
400 ml/14 fl oz/1¾ cups double
(heavy) cream
sea salt

This ridiculously named recipe is one of the more sensible dishes from Salvador Dalí's cookbook *Les Diners de Gala*. As it's easy to imagine, Dalí's cookbook is somewhat light in instruction on how to actually make anything. This is partially because all the recipes come from the great French restaurants so, from one chef to another, it was obvious what was going on. This dish is from La Tour d'Argent and there are some wonderful photos of Dalí at the restaurant with the chef, the maître d' and "the bush".

Back on Planet Earth we had to deconstruct the dish to work out how it could be made and served. There are two components: the bush of crayfish and the crayfish *fumet*. The suggestion is that you look at the bush while you sup on the *fumet*. It makes sense but doesn't quite do it for us. In reality once your guests are well lubricated and with a bit encouragement they will pull apart the bush and eat that too. Aïoli is a good thing to have on hand for when this happens (it may not be at the same time as the supping but we can guarantee you that it will happen sooner or later). Live crayfish are surprisingly cute – they are exactly like mini lobsters, but they can be vicious so treat them gently. One more thing, "Viking herbs" just means chopped dill...

Prepare the *fumet* the day before. Add all the *fumet* ingredients (except the dill) to a large pan and bringing to the boil. Once boiling, reduce the heat and simmer for 20 minutes, then take off the heat, add the dill and leave to infuse for an hour or so.

Strain the stock, bring it back to the boil and add the crayfish in batches of 20. Fortunately, as the crayfish are so dinky, they only last a couple of seconds before they give up, unlike lobsters, which can thrash around for what seems like ages. Cover with a lid and simmer for about 7 minutes. Remove with a sieve (strainer) and leave to cool on a tray. While you cook the remaining crayfish you can get to work removing the meat from the cooked ones.

Choose the best looking 40 crayfish and set them aside whole. For the remaining crayfish, turn them on their backs, hold in both hands and twist off the tails. Put the head aside and then carefully remove the meat from the tails by pulling the armour apart. It is sensible to wear gloves to protect your hands. Keep the shells.

(continues overleaf)

You should be left with 40 whole crayfish, about 60 pieces of tail meat, a bowlful of shells and a graveyard of clawed heads.

When everything is cool, refrigerate everything except the shells.

Put the *fumet* into a jug (pitcher). Wipe out the large pan, add the olive oil and, when hot, add the shells, sautéing them to remove excess moisture, about 3 minutes. Turn the heat down and add the onion and celery and cook, without browning, until soft. Turn up the heat and add the Cognac, cooking until most of the liquid has gone. Add the tomatoes and do the same deglazing trick. Finally, add the vermouth and continue cooking until it has reduced in volume by half.

Pass the soup through a very fine sieve or chinois then strain through a clean tea (dish) towel set over a sieve. If you want to go to town you could clarify the soup but it is probably one labour too far. Chill until ready to serve.

To assemble the bush
To make the bush you will need to create a framework for the crayfish to be attached to.

FOR THE TOWER
1 piece of thin (eg 4 mm/ ¹/₆ in) plywood or MDF, about 24 x 28 cm/9¹/₂ x 11 in
hand saw (or rail saw)
orange gaffer tape
staple gun and staples

Crayfish support tower
Start by marking out the wood. For 40 crayfish you don't need a huge bush. Mark out three isosceles triangles, 12 cm/4 in wide x 28 cm/11 in high and carefully cut them out. Use the gaffer tape to stick the triangles together to make a pyramid. Cover the remaining wood with more gaffer tape for a uniform surface. Orange tape is a bonus, if you can get it, if not black is second best.

Now, using the staple gun, attach the crayfish upside down, stapling through their tails. For details of arrangement look at the photo on p.83. Start at the bottom and work your way up each side. This way staples will be hidden as the crayfish overlap. It's best to attach the crayfish immediately before you serve it. Otherwise you should refrigerate the tower until it is needed. Place the tower on a fancy dish and decorate the crayfish with bunches of dill.

Reheat the *fumet* and add the cream. Adjust the seasoning with a little extra sea salt as necessary. Ceremoniously place the bush in the centre of the table and then serve the *fumet*.

CLAM CHOWDER/ CORN CHOWDER

Clam chowder is a popular and filling soup, the sort of thing to line your stomach ready for some hard feasting. It's economical to make because you don't need a whole load of clams. You can also adapt the recipe to make a dish that is more main course rather than soup. In this case get twice as many clams and thin the chowder with more milk to create a *moules mariniere*-style dish. It will look smart and be tasty to boot. The traditional accompaniment to the chowder is little oyster crackers, which translates to picking up a box of Ritz when you are in the supermarket.

If you can't get the clams, fresh corn cut off the cob and added near the end is delicious. Forego the bacon and you've got a vegetarian dish too.

SERVES 4

25 g/1 oz/1 tbsp butter
75 g/2³/₄ oz smoked bacon lardons (pieces)
75 g/2³/₄ oz celery
75 g/2³/₄ oz onion
75 g/2³/₄ oz potato, peeled
25 g/1 oz plain (all purpose) flour
800 ml/1¹/₂ pints/scant 3¹/₂ cups milk
100 ml/3¹/₂ fl oz/generous ¹/₃ cup double (heavy) cream
salt
500 g/1 lb 2 oz clams in their shells or 200 g/7 oz corn, cut from the cob (about 2 cobs worth)
chopped parsley, to serve

Find a roomy saucepan, add the butter and cook the bacon until cooked through but not brown. While this is happening chop the celery, onion and potato into equal 5-mm/¹/₄-in cubes. When the bacon is done, add the celery, onion and potato and cook gently in the butter until soft and translucent, putting back on a low heat once the pan has cooled down sufficiently to stop them scorching. Stir in the flour and cook for a few minutes to form a roux. Add the milk, bit by bit, and cook slowly until everything is combined, about 10 minutes.

Once the flour has cooked out you can chill this mix and come back to it nearer the time when you want to eat.

Add the cream and season with a little salt. Finally, about 5 minutes before you want to serve the dish add the clams (or corn) and cover the pan. It is ready when all of the clams have opened. Serve at once, sprinkled with chopped parsley.

MAINS

FISH

GRILLED SOLES WITH MÂITRE D'HÔTEL BUTTER

This is one of those old-fashioned dishes that is so simple it is hardly a recipe, yet it is ideal for an impressive main course. Depending on your budget you can either get lemon soles or larger Dover soles. See what is available when you go shopping. The only tricky bit of this dish is peeling the skin off the fish. You need the dark skin removed, but this is something that your fishmonger will do for you.

SERVES 8

FOR THE *MÂITRE D'HÔTEL* BUTTER
125 g/4 oz/1 stick/½ cup salted butter, cut into cubes
juice of ½ lemon
1 tbsp finely chopped parsley

FOR THE GRILLED SOLES
8 lemon soles
1 x recipe *maître d'hôtel* butter (see above)
50 g/1¾ oz/3½ tbsp butter, melted
parsley sprigs
4 tomatoes, to serve (optional)

Using a food mixer, beat the butter until it is soft, then mix in the lemon juice and parsley. Lay out a sheet of cling film (plastic wrap) and place the butter mixture in the middle. Pat out to create a sausage shape, about 12 cm/5 in long. Roll up in the cling film and twist the ends to create a smooth roll. Refrigerate until hardened.

At least half an hour before serving, remove the *maître d'hôtel* butter from the refrigerator and slice it into 8 rounds, about 8 mm/³⁄₈ in thick. Pop them on a plate and allow them to soften a little.

Brush a grill pan with some of the melted butter and lay the soles skin-side down on the pan. You will probably need to cook the soles in two batches. Brush some more butter on top and grill for about 5 minutes, or until the fish is cooked through. There is no need to turn them. Keep the soles warm at the bottom of the oven.

Line a large serving dish with a linen napkin. Arrange the soles on top and place a round of the *maître d'hôtel* butter on top of the fish. Arrange parsley sprigs between each fish. For extra fun cut some tomatoes in half using a zigzag series of cuts across the equator. Serve at once.

CREAMED SMOKED HADDOCK WITH BACON AND PEAS IN A VOL-AU-VENT

Even attempting to master the vol-au-vent is greatly satisfying. It's one of those things that you could spend your life perfecting but hopefully, even if you just follow our instructions, you should get a triumphant result on your first attempt. Go to p.211-3 to follow our technique.

Vol-au-vents are wonderfully old-fashioned but have been bastardized by the kind of people who offer "catering solutions". Like all good ideas this majestic pastry creation has a noble background, having been invented by Antonin Carême, our architectural pastry hero. The best fillings for vol-au-vents are invariably things that are bound with a creamy white sauce – just to reinforce that this dish is in no way good for you.

This recipe is great for feasting as everything can be done in advance and reheated just before serving. A food mixer is advisable when making the pastry. It's not impossible without, but it is a lot of work.

SERVES 8 AS A STARTER

1 x vol-au-vent case (see p.211-3)
100 g/3¹/₂ oz bacon
25 g/1 oz/2 tbsp butter
1 small onion, diced
1 bay leaf
25 g/1 oz/2 tbsp plain (all purpose) flour
600 ml/1 pint/2¹/₂ cups milk
100 ml/3¹/₂ fl oz/generous ¹/₃ cup double (heavy) cream
500 g/1 lb 2 oz smoked haddock
75 g/2³/₄ oz/scant ²/₃ cup frozen peas
chopped parsley, to serve

In a casserole dish or thick-bottomed saucepan, brown the bacon in the butter until crispy. Remove with a slotted spoon and drain on a piece of kitchen paper (paper towel). Set to one side. Now add the onion and the bay leaf, take the pan off the heat and stir so that the onion doesn't burn. By the time the fat has cooled a little the onion should be cooked through and translucent.

Put the pan back over a low heat and start adding the flour to the fat until all of the fat has been absorbed. Cook very gently for a couple of minutes, stirring constantly so that it doesn't catch. Add the milk slowly to the roux, keep stirring and cooking gently until you have created a white sauce. Next, add the cream and adjust the consistency and seasoning. It shouldn't be thin but at the same time you don't want it stodgy thick either. When everything is right add the smoked haddock and cook gently for about 10 minutes, or until the fish is hot and cooked through. Stir every so often so that it doesn't catch.

Fill your cooked vol-au-vent case with the mixture just before serving, sprinkled with parsley.

GET AHEAD: cook the white sauce in advance, then 20 minutes before serving reheat the sauce and add the fish and the peas.

FOWL

TROPICAL CHICKEN

"ONE WOULD EAT ONE'S OWN FATHER IN THIS SAUCE."
– GRIMOD DE LA REYNIÈRE –

Today you conquer chicken. This dish will get everyone's coconut cups flowing over. A trash epic of chicken, flavour and spices presented in a hollowed out pineapple. It evokes a tropical breeze, rainstorms and could lead to a magical night of a thousand drinks.

Be warned – eat too much and you'll develop a tangy meat sweat. The recipe is tasty and distending your stomach every once in a while can be fun so overindulgence is always tempting. If served for four you may like to lie down for a little while after dinner to sweat it out. Tropical!

SERVES 8

130 g/4$\frac{1}{2}$ oz ginger (peeled weight)
1 onion (about 180 g/6$\frac{1}{2}$ oz unpeeled)
1 head garlic
100 g/3$\frac{1}{2}$ oz lemon marmalade
100 ml/3$\frac{1}{2}$ fl oz/generous $\frac{1}{3}$ cup soy sauce
50 ml/1$\frac{3}{4}$ fl oz/scant $\frac{1}{4}$ cup white wine vinegar
2 free-range chickens
2 pineapples

First make the marinade. Mince the ginger, onion and peeled garlic cloves into a bowl. Stir in the marmalade and then the soy sauce and vinegar.

Next step is chopping up the chickens. You could get your butcher to do this for you but it's the kind of thing you should know how to do. With proper preparation the humble chicken will look much more comely when cooked. Lollipop the chicken legs and wings. See overleaf for the technique.

Place the chicken pieces in a dish and cover with the marinade. Give it a really good mix round. Wash your hands and cover the dish with clingfilm (plastic wrap). Refrigerate for a couple of hours, or longer if there's time.

Preheat the oven to 180°C/350°F/Gas Mark 4.

Tip the chicken pieces and marinade onto a baking tray lined with foil. Remove the breast pieces and put aside. Cook in the oven for about 30 minutes or until the pieces are dark brown and sticky. After 15 minutes, add the breast pieces.

Meanwhile, hollow out a couple of pineapples. Remove the tops and set aside. Then, using a paring knife, cut a deep cylinder into the pineapple. Poke the knife in at a few places where you think the bottom of the cylinder is and wiggle the knife. This cuts the base of the cylinder through, but keeps the pineapple intact. Lever out the cylinder of pineapple. Serve the chicken in the hollowed out pineapple, with coconut rice on the side.

QUAILS ROASTED WITH MARMALADE AND TOBACCO

This recipe is our secret weapon - an elegant stiletto dagger of a dish. It sounds sophisticated, but it's easy to cook and goes straight in for the kill.

We first developed it for the Barbican Art Gallery in London when they asked us to cook a surreal dinner for the launch of their Surreal House Exhibition. For the starter we served the smells of rubber, wintergreen and mothballs all set to the film *Steamboat Bill*. The next course needed to do a bit more for peoples' stomachs. It was time to get meaty. The main course starred mounds of these crispy and sticky quails perfumed with a hit of tobacco.

Quail is very forgiving so the recipe scales up easily. With the right equipment you can cook for hundreds and hold the quails for a good long time without destroying the flavour and texture.

SERVES 4 AMPLY
groundnut (peanut) oil, for oiling
1 bunch of thyme, roughly chopped
1 handful of rosemary, roughly chopped
1 tsp Maldon salt
1 tsp black peppercorns, crushed
340 g/12 oz Seville orange marmalade
juice of 1 lemon
juice of 1 orange
20 ml/4 tsp tobacco syrup (see Suppliers)
8 quails

Oil a baking tray and massage all the ingredients into the birds. Roast in a hot oven until crisp and well cooked, about 25 minutes, basting regularly with the sticky sauce.

Serve, mounded into a pyramid, with mashed potatoes and a fennel and Pernod salad. Encourage your guests to eat with their fingers. Finger bowls are sensible.

CAPED TURKEY

Clothing for food is very practical. The insulating cape keeps the bird nice and warm and stops it drying out, so it's like foil, but with much more effort required.

Roast the turkey in the traditional way. This is not the time to start de-limbing the bird and cooking cuts separately in search of tenderness. Just cook it according to what it says on the pack. For extra fun we like to force a pack of butter between the flesh and the skin of the breast.

FOR THE TURKEY CAPE
500 x 500 mm/20 x 20 in piece of fabric for top
600 x 500 mm/24 x 20 in piece of Mylar or foil for underside
enough braiding to run around the edges and form drawstrings

When making the cape you will need 2 pieces of fabric. The outer one is what your guests will see, whereas the one below performs as a reflective layer to keep the bird warm. We've used a gold padded fabric for the top layer, but you can use whatever you like. For the underside, Mylar (the plastic reflective foil that keeps marathon runners warm) is an ideal choice. Tin foil is also possible but is a little more tricky to sew and keep in one piece.

Use a large piece of paper to make a simple pattern for the cape. Check that it fits over your bird. Cut out the fabric and the Mylar, layer them up and then sew together with the braiding. Extend the braiding out so that you can tie it around the bird.

As a festive alternative, a waistcoat and bowtie is always smart.

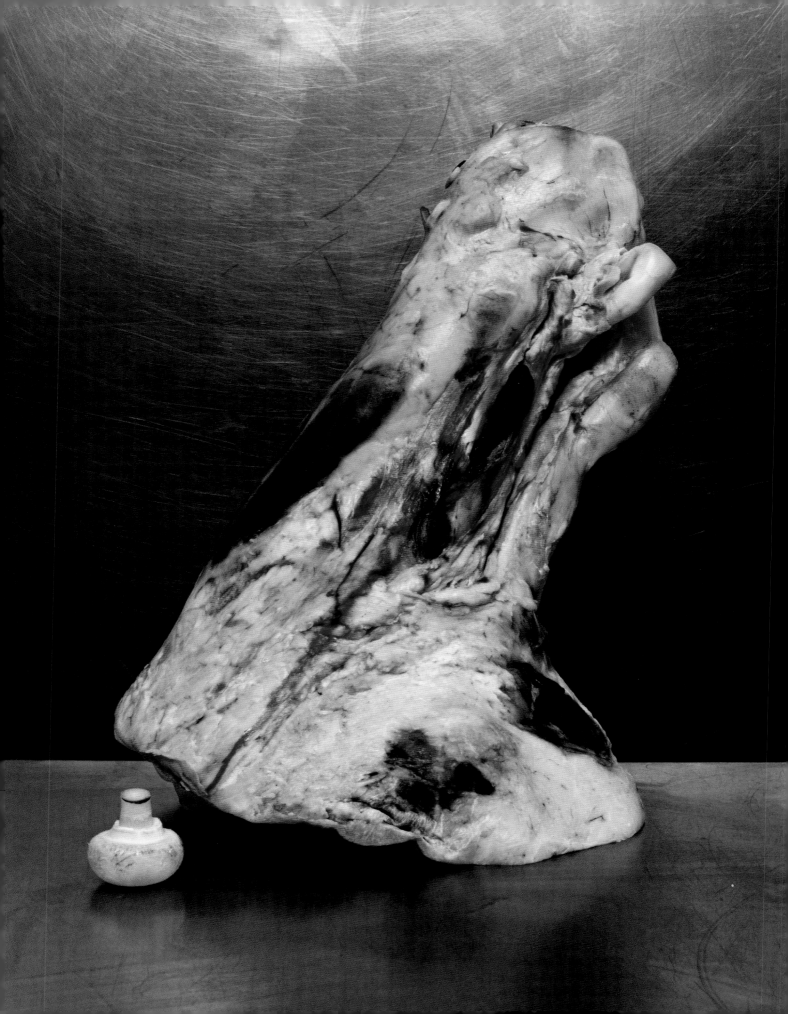

MEAT

GLITTER HAM

TO COOK THE HAM
1 bone-in gammon
(about 6 kg/13 lb 4 oz)
2 celery sticks
1 carrot, peeled
1 onion, cut in half
8 black peppercorns
1 bay leaf

FOR THE GLITTER HAM
340 g/12 oz jar of marmalade,
without bits
50 ml/1³/₄ fl oz/scant ¹/₄ cup whisky
50 g/1³/₄ oz/¹/₄ cup brown sugar
1 precooked and cooled ham,
trimmed (see above)
edible glitter

We don't believe in strict vegetarianism – you have canine teeth for a reason. The Aiello-Wheeler hypothesis (also known as the "expensive tissue hypothesis") is its own compelling argument for omnivory. You may be surprised, however, that we enjoy cooking for vegetarians. Most of them have been let down so many times by disappointing and lame vegetarian offers at restaurants that they are not difficult to impress. A simple cheese fondue served in a customized pineapple has done the trick on a couple of occasions.

This dish takes the same principles of an outrageous garnish and applies them to meat. Of course it is American. The world's first "glitter ham" appears on the Martha Stewart show where a puckish Conan O'Brian covers a festive ham in gold. Disappointingly Martha tells viewers, "this is inedible gold – don't get any ideas." With a bit of application though you can make one that's good enough to eat.

Cake shops sell edible gold dust but this can look flat. What you want is edible glitter, which comes in a variety of colours to suit all bad tastes. Glittering the ham is straightforward. The ham needs to be cold, so you can either cook your own ham in advance or buy one ready cooked.

Glitter ham is a wild accompaniment to the traditional Christmas bird. Sam's girlfriend (an illustrator and art director) suggests covering My Little Ponies in unashamed glitter and using them for name places.

Soak the gammon, overnight if necessary (ask your butcher). Alternatively, bring to the boil and throw out the water. Place the gammon in a large pot, throw in the aromatics and cover with water. Bring to the boil, cover and simmer for about 4 hours. If you have a digital probe thermometer cook the ham until it reaches 80°C/176°F. Allow the ham to cool slightly, then remove it from the broth. The resulting stock can be used to make an excellent soup.

The next task is to carefully remove the skin from the ham. It should easily peel off. Spend a few minutes neatening up the remaining layer of fat with a sharp knife.

Start by making the glaze. In a small saucepan, boil up the marmalade, whisky and sugar until it becomes sticky. Use a brush to paint the glaze all over the ham (don't bother with the bottom). Carefully sprinkle the entire ham with the edible glitter until it is evenly covered. Transfer the ham to a serving platter, being careful not to disturb the glitter. Slice and serve with Cumberland sauce.

PULLED PORK

Pulled pork is a regular in our studio. You can put it on in the morning and then forget about it until lunchtime. We like to use the Momofuku rub: equal quantities of salt and sugar, which gives the meat a particularly fine taste. Pork belly is the proper cut for this one. Make sure you buy decent meat as it really makes such a difference. At the moment we like pork from the Middle White pig. Cook this up and feast like an ogre on a sizzling mound of meat.

SERVES 8
50 g/1³/₄ oz/¹/₄ cup caster (superfine) sugar
50 g/1³/₄ oz sea salt
3 kg/6 lb 8 oz piece pork belly, scored

Mix the sugar and salt together and rub all over the belly. Place on a tray and cover with cling film (plastic wrap). Refrigerate for a few hours. As time passes the salt will draw out some moisture, which can be drained off. You can do this curing a day ahead if you need to. If you run out of time and just rub and cook it's not the end of the world either.

Preheat the oven to 220°C/425°F/Gas Mark 7.

Roast the belly skin side up in the oven for 45 minutes. You should get a lot of browning, and a fair amount of fat will render out. Turn the oven down to 150°C/300°F/Gas Mark 2 and continue to cook for another 1¹/₂ hours. If you need to you can cook the pork the day before and then reheat it in the oven for an hour.

Place the slab of meat on a salver and invite guests to pull the meat apart.

BRAISED BEEF SHIN

Beef shin is a magnificent cut – it's got a bone of epic proportions, it's inexpensive and becomes meltingly tender with ease. Your butcher will be happy to procure a shin bone for you. Ask him to leave the meat on the bone. For this recipe about 4 kg/8 lb 13 oz of meat is ideal. This works out as about half the shin. If you are cooking for more people you can get the entire shin but you'll need to cook it in the oven – make sure you can fit it in! It's big and nasty.

SERVES 8

4 kg/8 lb 13 oz piece of beef shin, bone in
2 star anise
2 onions, cut in half
1 bay leaf
8 black peppercorns
sea salt
2 celery sticks
1 carrot

Place the shin bone in a casserole or large saucepan, add the aromatics and top up with water. Bring slowly to the boil, skimming off any scum and then turn down to a gentle simmer and cover with a lid. You can either place in a low oven for about 3 hours, or continue to cook on the stove over a very low heat. The meat is ready when the bone is sticking out proud and the meat is on the verge of falling apart.

Carefully remove the meat from the pot. If the meat is very delicate it may be easier to drain the stock off first. Lift the meat, bone aloft onto a serving dish and serve with buttered greens and mashed potatoes.

COW PIE

In the pantheon of literary debauches the account of Trimalchio's feast rates pretty highly. It is an episode that appears in Petronius' first-century satire, *Satyricon*. Guests eat through a series of choreographed surprises including monster's eggs, unguents raining from the ceiling, a 200 pound boiled calf wearing a helmet, exploding cakes, *memento mori* and a surprise visit from the fire brigade. This sounds like a great deal of fun but there are easier (and tastier) ways to create spectacle at the table. This pie with rampant marrow bone does the trick, providing all the theatre needed for a glorious main dish.

SERVES 8

Preheat the oven to 160°C/315°F/Gas Mark 2–3.

FOR THE FILLING
25 g/1 oz/2 tbsp butter
2 tbsp groundnut (peanut) oil
800 g/1 lb 12 oz stewing steak, diced
200 g/7 oz ox kidney, diced
4 small onions, peeled and diced
6 thyme sprigs, picked
1 small garlic clove, peeled and finely chopped
30 g/1 oz/2 tbsp plain (all-purpose) flour
250 ml/9 fl oz/generous 1 cup beef stock
20 ml/¾ fl oz/4 tsp Worcestershire sauce
100 ml/3½ fl oz/scant ½ cup ale
salt and black pepper
1 marrow bone

Melt the butter and oil together in a large pan over a high heat. When hot add the beef in a few batches to brown all over. Use a slotted spoon to remove the meat to a colander sitting on top of a plate. Add the kidney and brown briefly before removing from the pan. When all the beef is done and out of the pan turn the heat down to low and sweat off the onions until soft. Add the thyme and garlic and cook for a couple of minutes longer. Add the flour to the pan and mix carefully making sure not to leave any lumps. When the flour is mixed in add the stock, Worcestershire sauce and ale. Bring to a low simmer, cover and cook for an hour. Adjust the seasoning with salt and pepper.

While this is cooking, get on with making the pastry (dough). Sift the flour into the bowl of a food mixer fitted with a metal mixing blade. Dice the butter and mix through the flour. Add the salt and mix on a low speed until the butter is broken down into tiny crumbs and dispersed thoroughly with the flour.

FOR THE PASTRY (PIE DOUGH)
500 g/1 lb 2 oz/3½ cups plain (all-purpose) flour, plus extra for dusting
250 g/9 oz/1⅛ cups butter
salt
130 ml/4½ fl oz/generous ½ cup water
1 egg yolk
1 tbsp double (heavy) cream

With the motor running, add the water a splash at a time to bring the mixture together. You may need more or less water depending on the weather. On a lightly floured surface, work the pastry for a few minutes to bring it all together then wrap in cling film (plastic wrap) and refrigerate for half an hour.

Roll the dough out so that it is about 0.5 cm/¼ in thick. Find a suitably sized pie dish and line the dish with the dough, carefully removing excess with a knife. Rework the remaining dough and roll out the lid. Fill the pie making sure that the beef is evenly distributed. Place the marrow bone in the centre of the pie using the meat to position it in place. Cut a cross slit in the middle of the lid and lift carefully over the top, poking the bone through and then onto the dish. Use extra slivers of dough to cover any gaps around the bone joint. Brush the lid with a mixture of egg yolk and double (heavy) cream and cook in the oven for about 50 minutes.

MEDIEVAL ROAST BEEF

Jabbing a blade through several chunks of meat and nursing them over an open flame is one of the oldest forms of cookery known to man. It's also something that the English have always excelled in. The other is jelly.

It was Ivan Day, food historian and our culinary hero, that first introduced us to proper roasting. He's got all the kit, including a cannon ball-powered spit. The idea is to suspend the meat in front of the fire and have it slowly turn.

It's not too hard to improvise a basic spit at home. Obviously you will need a fire going. In the past we've used a fire poker, given it a good clean and speared a rolled topside with it. Prop it up on some bricks and set it about half a metre/just under 2 feet back from a glowing fire. It's difficult to give timings as it depends on so many things. But it's not particularly fast, so allow at least a couple of hours for a smallish joint.

In order to test for doneness of the meat we like to use a little skewer trick. Get a metal skewer and push it into the centre of the meat. Leave it for exactly five seconds. Immediately place the skewer on your bottom lip. If the skewer burns you, the meat is really overdone. If it feels cold then no heat has reached the centre so it need more cooking. If it feels a little warm then the meat is rare. It takes a bit of practice to know what feeling equates to each stage but as you practice you will get the hang of it, or just go and buy an instant-read thermometer.

DESSERT

TECHRON TRIFLE — A STIMULANT TRIFLE

It's good to finish a meal with a rip-roaring finale. We like to create a centrifugal centrepiece that captures the kind of awe we have probably all experienced when contemplating the wonders of outer space, strange bioluminescent deep sea fish or the architecture of the human body. Hard to do with a single dish, but a well constructed trifle can get you some of the way there.

Our stimulant trifle is turbo-charged for maximum impact. It's a nuclear dessert on steroids, a berserker version of one of the noblest British puddings.

It was first presented with a trifle-based performance at the Serpentine gallery in London. The art gallery was hosting an all-nighter where guests learnt about sleep disorders, dreams, time and some art. These are big concepts so we developed a dish with a galaxy of uppers and downers that could help visitors stay awake all night and muscle through it.

On the stroke of midnight, a parade of 20 servers, robed in white gowns and armed with spears and candles, processed into the gallery bearing a white haired maiden aloft on a large metal shield. She was carrying a trifle big enough to feed 120 in a single sitting. We had tried to get hold of a troop of white horses with mounted kettledrums from the local cavalry regiment. The Blues and Royals are barracked next to the gallery. However, their troopers were being deployed to Afghanistan the next day (with tanks not horses) so we made do with what we could get hold of.

The parade helped make the trifle a sensation. The strong entrance created a moment of awe before a fruity young gallerist led the charge to eat. In minutes it became feral and people got Victorian on this traditional, creamy dessert.

Good processions need epic music. We regularly use Michael Nyman's *Memorial* from the final scene of *The Cook, The Thief, His Wife and Her Lover*. As it is over 11 minutes long, you have a chance to sort out any last minute technical hitches. When picking a walk-on song look to the experts. Politicians and wrestlers are adept at using music to hype the crowd as they enter the arena.

(recipe continues overleaf)

FOR THE LIME AND ABSINTHE JELLY

100 ml/3½ fl oz/generous ⅓ cup lime juice

100 ml/3½ fl oz/generous ⅓ cup sugar syrup

50 ml/1¾ fl oz/scant ¼ cup absinthe

250 ml/9 fl oz/generous 1 cup water

FOR THE WHIPPED CREAM

120 ml/4 fl oz/½ cup double (heavy) cream

FOR THE ETHER CUSTARD

8 egg yolks

50 g/1¾ oz/¼ cup caster (superfine) sugar

2 tsp cornflour (cornstarch)

600 ml/1 pint/2½ cups double (heavy) cream

1 ml ether

FOR THE PINEAPPLE AND ABSINTHE JAM

2 medium-sized pineapples

sugar

juice of 2 limes

50 ml/1¾ fl oz/scant ¼ cup absinthe

FOR THE BOUDOIR BISCUITS

about 20 biscuits (see recipe on p.137)

TO DECORATE (OPTIONAL)

Peeled and sliced kiwi fruit

Free cigarettes (on cocktail sticks, stuck into the top of a pineapple)

For the lime and absinthe jelly

Combine all the ingredients and set using 5 gelatine leaves. For detailed jelly making tips see pp.122–4. Pour the jelly into 10 small moulds and place in the refrigerator to set.

For the whipped cream

Whip the double (heavy) cream using a food mixer or hand-held beaters. Refrigerate until needed.

For the ether custard

In a heatproof bowl, whisk the egg yolks with the sugar and cornflour (cornstarch). Heat the cream until it is scalding then pour over the egg yolks, stirring vigorously as you do so. Place the bowl over a pan of simmering water. Stir the mixture until it thickens. Once cool, refrigerate. Stir in the ether shortly before assembling the trifle.

For the pineapple and absinthe jam

Peel, core and eye the pineapples, then chop finely, trying to save as much of the juice as possible. Have a bowl ready on the scales. Weigh the chopped pineapple and add an equal quantity of sugar, then add the lime juice. Cover with cling film (plastic wrap) and refrigerate overnight.

Next day, transfer the sugary fruit to a pan and boil rapidly until a set is achieved. Use a refrigerator cold plate to test it. Finally, stir in the absinthe.

To assemble the trifle

Find the biggest trifle bowl you have. Any suitably sized glass vessel is normally a winner. Start by layering in the boudoir biscuits along the bottom and sides, sprinkling with absinthe as you go, then spoon in half the jam trying to spread it evenly over the biscuits. Add sliced absinthe jellies and kiwi fruit around the perimeter. Hold them in place using half the ether custard and then half the whipped cream. Repeat with more jam, then custard, finishing with a big mound of cream on top. Place the top of a pineapple (studded with cigarettes if wished) in the centre of the trifle. Unmould the jellies and place them around.

ICE CREAM MÉLANGE

Since meeting a six year old in Australia who only ate (the always challenging) blue food, we've been working our way through the spectrum trying to achieve the ultimate colours in our food.

Sybaritic roman emperor Nero was similarly interested in colour and food. As well as being a populist who, Suetonius says, "showed neither discrimination nor moderation in putting to death whomsoever he pleased" he was both a gourmet and gourmand. Archeologists have dug up an ancient revolving dining room he used to entertain guests in, and one of his party tricks (besides persecuting Christians) was to serve monochromatic meals.

Focusing your energies on colour is a good way to explore the boundaries of culinary creativity. Dessert is the proper place to do this as there's a bit more leeway in terms of playfulness and whimsy. Purples and greys are appetite suppressants, while oranges, yellows and reds prepare you to eat.

Start your own experiments in chromatic dining with these tasty ice cream recipes and colour them to please the eye and tongue.

FOR THE ICE-CREAM BASE
3 egg yolks
100 g/3$\frac{1}{2}$ oz/$\frac{1}{2}$ cup granulated sugar
300 ml/10 fl oz/1$\frac{1}{4}$ cups whole milk
250 ml/9 fl oz/generous 1 cup double (heavy) cream

For the ice cream base

In a heatproof bowl large enough to take the milk and cream, whisk together the yolks and sugar until they are pale. An electric blender is a good thing here.

Meanwhile, bring the milk and cream up to a simmer, then pour over the yolks and sugar mix, whisking further so that everything is incorporated. Place the bowl over a pan of simmering water and stir from time to time until the custard thickens, about 20 minutes. It won't thicken massively but it will be enough so that when you place a clean wooden spoon in the mixture and draw a line, the line stays put. If you have a thermometer cook the mixture until it reaches 85°C/185°F.

As soon as the base is cooked pour it into a metal bowl set over ice and stir periodically until it is cool. The mixture will keep for a couple of days refrigerated before it needs to be churned.

(continues overleaf)

ICE CREAM MÉLANGE

FOR PINEAPPLE ICE CREAM

1 pineapple

300 g/10½ oz/1½ cups sugar

300 ml/10 fl oz/1¼ cups water

1 recipe ice-cream base (see p.117)

yellow food colouring

**FOR GRENADINE RIPPLE
ICE CREAM**

2 pomegranates

100 g/3½ oz/½ cup sugar

1 recipe ice-cream base (see p.117)

FOR MINT ICE CREAM

1 small bunch of mint leaves

1 recipe ice-cream base (see p.117)

green food colouring

For pineapple ice cream

Peel and core the pineapple. Cut into dice, place in a small saucepan and add the sugar and water. Bring to the boil and simmer gently for 45 minutes. Strain the pineapple and blend in a food processor until it is pulped, then strain through a fine sieve (strainer). The remaining pineapple syrup can be put to good use in Alchemical Mountain Brew on p.166.

Add the pineapple pulp to the ice-cream base, add a touch of yellow food colouring and churn in an ice-cream machine until thick.

For grenadine ripple ice cream

Cut the pomegranates in half and squeeze until there is 200 ml/7 fl oz/ generous ¾ cup of juice. Strain and keep back the seeds. Add the sugar to the juice and boil rapidly in a small pan until you have a thick syrup, about 5 minutes. Cool.

Churn the ice cream base mix in an ice-cream machine and, when it has turned into soft ice cream, stir in the pomegranate syrup. Use the saved seeds as a decoration for serving.

For mint ice cream

The trick with this is to infuse the mint in the milk and cream as you make the ice cream base. Then away you go. Add a touch of green food colouring just before churning the mix. To reverse engineer this you can buy mint choc chip flavourings – it's not that you shouldn't use it (it's probably been in any mint ice cream you have ever eaten), it's just that it somewhat defeats the point of home cooking.

BANANA FLAMBÉ

PER PERSON
1 banana
25 g/1 oz/¹⁄₈ cup caster (superfine) sugar
25 g/1 oz/2 tbsp butter
1 orange
35 ml/1¹⁄₄ fl oz/heaping 2 tbsp rum

The mysteries and delights of the dessert trolley are sadly no longer used to bring meals to a rabble-rousing climax. In the 1990s they were deemed too unfashionable and impractical for restaurants and so scrapped. Restaurateurs worked out they could stuff more covers into a dining room by putting the tables closer together, thereby increasing earnings per square foot. Though admirably businesslike this misses the romance, spectacle and excitement of a well-endowed dessert trolley forging towards you for a pumping grand finale.

Banana flambé served from a dessert trolley ends the meal with a cloud of banana fragrance and a blaze of glory. This flamboyant dessert lights up the table, puts a smile on people's faces and is a performance in it's own right.

We like to invoke Josephine Baker, showgirl, French resistance fighter, rights activist, winner of the Croix de Guerre and banana dancer, when flaming bananas. She charmed the globe with a skirt of fake bananas, a powerful voice, sexulous dancing and sheer brio. When we do our flaming banana routine we try to capture her energy and fully exploit the comedic and libidinous potential of the banana.

The flaming bananas can be served with your mélange of ice creams (see pp.117–9).

Peel the banana and slice in half along its length. Heat a frying pan and add the sugar and butter. When the two have started to form a light caramel add the bananas, flat side down. Slowly jiggle the pan to make sure that the caramel cooks evenly. Squeeze in a little orange juice.

Have ready the rum and carefully pour it into the pan, making sure that it's away from any flames. Now either tip the pan towards the flame to set the rum alight or light the rum with a match. The flames will go wild for a few seconds and then die down.

Serve the bananas with ice cream and boudoir biscuits (see p.137).

RAINBOW JELLY

SERVES 16

FOR THE SUGAR SYRUP

300 g/10$\frac{1}{2}$ oz/1$\frac{1}{2}$ cups granulated sugar

600 ml/1 pint/2$\frac{1}{2}$ cups boiling water

FOR THE LIME JELLY

250 ml/9 fl oz/generous 1 cup lime juice

100 ml/3$\frac{1}{2}$ fl oz/generous $\frac{1}{3}$ cup water

150 ml/5 fl oz/$\frac{2}{3}$ cup sugar syrup

5 gelatine leaves

FOR THE COCONUT BLANCMANGE

200 ml /7 fl oz/generous $\frac{3}{4}$ cup Vita coconut water

150 ml/5 fl oz/$\frac{2}{3}$ cup rice milk

100 ml/3$\frac{1}{2}$ fl oz/generous $\frac{1}{3}$ cup cardamom-infused sugar syrup (see note in sugar syrup method)

50 ml/1$\frac{3}{4}$ fl oz/scant $\frac{1}{2}$ cup water

5 gelatine leaves

FOR THE MANGO JELLY

2 passion fruit

210 ml/7fl oz/$\frac{3}{4}$ cup mango juice

100 ml/3$\frac{1}{3}$ fl oz/generous $\frac{1}{3}$ cup orange juice

30 ml/2 tbsp lemon juice

130 ml/4$\frac{1}{2}$ fl oz/$\frac{1}{2}$ cup sugar syrup

5 gelatine leaves

FOR THE POMEGRANATE JELLY

$\frac{1}{2}$ pomegranate

210 ml/7fl oz/$\frac{3}{4}$ cup pomegranate juice

30 ml/2 tbsp orange juice

20 ml/4 tsp lemon juice

100 ml/3$\frac{1}{2}$ fl oz/$\frac{1}{3}$ cup sugar syrup

120 ml/4 fl oz/ $\frac{1}{2}$ cup water

5 gelatine leaves

A jelly that celebrates fruit and delves into Carmen Miranda's headdress for inspiration. We first served this striped jelly as dessert for "A Visionary Feast"; a seven-course banquet screening of *A Holy Mountain* by Alejandro Jodorowsky.

All the jelly recipes can be made in the same way up to 500 ml/17 fl oz/ generous 2 cups. You will have enough for two striped 1-litre/1$\frac{3}{4}$-pint/4-cup moulds. Do not be intimidated by the five layer set, we wholly recommend some cans of Red Stripe lager and righteous reggae tunes to pass the time. Alternatively, the addition of 100 ml/3$\frac{1}{2}$ fl oz/generous $\frac{1}{3}$ cup of light rum, or yellow chartreuse and an extra leaf of gelatine will make each of the recipes stand-alone jellies.

Makes enough for 2 litres/3$\frac{1}{2}$ pints/8 cups of jelly.

For the sugar syrup

Begin by making a batch of simple sugar syrup, which can be used for all the fruit jellies.

Combine 300 g/10$\frac{1}{2}$ oz/1$\frac{1}{2}$ cups of sugar with 600 ml/1 pint/2$\frac{1}{2}$ cups of boiling water and stir until completely dissolved.

Infusing syrup: For the coconut blancmange, the syrup can be made separately; add 10 bashed cardamom pods to the boiling water to add flavour.

For the jellies

Start with the top layer of lime jelly. Combine all the ingredients except the gelatine. Cut the gelatine into a few pieces and place in a heatproof bowl. Add a few tablespoons of the jelly mixture so that the gelatine is just covered and let the gelatine soften for 10 minutes while you bring a small pan of water to a simmer. Place the bowl of softened gelatine over the simmering water and stir from time to time until it's totally dissolved.

Pour the remainder of the lime jelly mixture over the dissolved gelatine and stir to combine. Finally, pour the mixture through a sieve (strainer) into a jug (pitcher) and fill the mould to a depth of 2.5 cm/1 inch. Place in the refrigerator.

Make up the coconut blancmange and mango and pomegranate jellies following the same steps. By this point your lime jelly will be completely set. Add the second layer, the coconut blancmange in a finer stripe, about 1.5 cm/$\frac{5}{8}$ in and return the mould to the refrigerator. (continues overleaf)

In the meantime, begin to quickset your mango jelly. Fill a wide metal bowl with ice, place a metal bowl filled with the mango jelly mixture on top and stir continuously for 5-10 minutes. As the mixture thickens add the seeds of 2 passion fruit so they combine evenly through and don't float to the surface. This will drastically reduce the total setting time for the whole jelly. When the coconut layer is firm enough add this golden elixir, and place back in the refrigerator.

Use the coconut blancmange for a fine white third layer and return to the refrigerator. This will dramatically offset the jewel-like pomegranate jelly embellished with the fruit seeds.

For the final pomegranate layer, add the seeds of $\frac{1}{2}$ a pomegranate to your jelly mixture and quickset over ice as you did with the passion fruit in the mango jelly. Pour your final layer into the mould and then return the finished jelly to the refrigerator.

Note: The art of layer building requires patience and attention to temperature. Be careful to ensure that the liquid jelly when added to the soft set layers is cool enough, so you don't melt an existing layer. Be as elaborate in layering as you have time.

NEON MARBLED JELLY

SERVES 16

FOR THE LIME JELLY MARBLE

200 ml/7 fl oz/generous ³/₄ cup lime
juice
150 ml/5 fl oz/²/₃ cup sugar syrup
(see p.122)
5 gelatine leaves

FOR THE CAMPARI AND ORANGE
JELLY MARBLE

150 ml/5 fl oz/²/₃ cup Campari
150 ml/5 fl oz/²/₃ cup orange peel
infused sugar syrup (see note on
p.122 about infusing)
50 ml/1³/₄ fl oz/scant ¹/₄ cup water
5 gelatine leaves

FOR THE MINT JELLY MARBLE

200 ml/7 fl oz/generous ³/₄ cup
boiling water (infused with a hand
full of fresh mint)
150 ml/5 fl oz/²/₃ cup sugar syrup
(see p.122)
5 gelatine leaves

FOR THE GIN JELLY BASE

250 ml/9 fl oz/generous 1 cup gin
200 ml/7 fl oz/generous ³/₄ cup
vermouth
50 ml/1³/₄ fl oz/scant ¹/₄ cup Campari
200 ml/7 fl oz/generous ³/₄ cup
orange peel infused sugar syrup (see
above)
250 ml/9 fl oz/generous 1 cup water
25 ml/2 tbsp lime juice
7 gelatine leaves
2 leaves of edible gold leaf or edible
glitter, to decorate

This neon marbled jelly takes the technique up a gear from our first jelly book.

Cocktails are good starting points to create ideas for the marbling. The trick is to deconstruct the main flavours in a cocktail to create loud jellied cubes bound with a clear or pastel-tinted alcoholic base jelly.

Marbling is either methodical or abstract – the jellied pieces could be coiled strips, circles or shapes. Choose up to four jelly flavours and use the palest in colour, with an alcoholic base and a more translucent set, to bind the cubes.

This recipe is a fruity take on a Negroni cocktail. Make contrasting jelly cubes in mint, orange and Campari and lime. These will be the marble elements. This recipe uses less water to make more intense flavoured pieces, and slightly more gelatine than usual to aid cutting and ensure a firmer cube.

Start by making all three jellies for marbling (lime, mint, Campari and orange). The extra gelatine in the recipe will help it set quickly. Pour the jellies into small trays so that the jelly is about 1 cm/¹/₂ in thick and chill. When set remove from the refrigerator and unmould using a sink of warm water. Tip the jellies onto a chopping (cutting) board and cut into even-sized cubes.

Make up the gin-based jelly. Double-strain it to ensure the mixture's transparency. Place the mixture in a metal bowl over a bowl of ice and stir to help it thicken quickly. As the mixture thickens add 2 leaves of gold leaf with a fork and agitate until there are flecks through out. Alternatively, use a teaspoon of edible glitter. Slowly incorporate a mixture of the coloured jelly cubes and fold gently through. Fill you mould, tap it a few times to get an even fill and refrigerate until set.

A note on glitter

Trash, glitz and elegance – we use edible glitter to create a multitude of effects. Use sparingly on top of cocktail jellies for party decadence or incorporate into layers by quicksetting over ice to go all out. There are a rainbow of colours available, from acid neons to pearlized pastels, that are visible in even the darkest blackcurrant jelly.

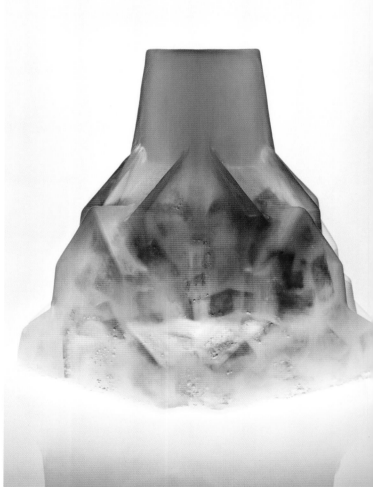

CORAL JELLY

SERVES 16

FOR THE CRANBERRY PEACH MARBLE

500 g/1 lb 2 oz cranberries
3 peaches
300 ml/10 fl oz/1¼ cups water
75 g/2½ oz/generous ⅓ cup sugar
1 star anise
100 ml/3½ fl oz/generous ⅓ cup sugar syrup (see p.122)
75 ml/2½ fl oz/5 tbsp water
15 ml/1 tbsp lemon juice
gelatine leaves (see recipe)

FOR THE JELLY BASE

300 ml/10 fl oz/1¼ cups gin
100 ml/3½ fl oz/generous ⅓ cup water
75 ml/2½ fl oz/5 tbsp créme de pêche de vigne
75 ml/2½ fl oz/5 tbsp lime juice
75 ml/2½ fl oz/5 tbsp blue Curaçao
50 ml/1¾ fl oz/scant ¼ cup sugar syrup (see p.122)
10 ml/2 tsp orange bitters
7 gelatine leaves

Begin by making the cranberry peach jelly used for the marbling. Wash the cranberries, finely slice the peaches and add to a saucepan. Add the water, sugar syrup and star anise. Bring to the boil and cover. Simmer until the cranberries are really soft. This takes about 30 minutes.

Line a sieve (strainer) with a clean tea (dish) towel and set over a bowl. Decant the fruits to the sieve and let the juice work its way through. You'll be left with a beautiful coral juice. To this, add the lemon juice.

Measure the volume of the fruit juice, and add 1 gelatine leaf for every 100 ml/3½ fl oz/generous ⅓ cup of liquid, and 1 extra leaf to allow easy cutting into cubes once set. This jelly should be intense to compliment the use of the gin in the binding mixture. Cut the gelatine leaves into a few pieces and place in a heatproof bowl. Add a few tablespoons of the jelly mixture so that the gelatine is just covered. Let the gelatine soften for 10 minutes while you bring a small pan of water to a simmer, then place the bowl of softened gelatine over the simmering water and stir from time to time until totally dissolved.

Pour the remainder of the marble mixture over the dissolved gelatine and stir to combine. Finally, pour the mixture through a sieve into a jug (pitcher). Use a clean shallow tray or cake tin (pan) to set this jelly and put in the refrigerator. It should set within an hour.

Remove from the refrigerator and unmould by placing the tray or tin in a sink of warm water to loosen. Turn out onto a chopping (cutting) board and use a knife to carefully cut into cube pieces.

While the marble element is setting, make up the jelly base and balance until happy with the sweetness and depth of flavour. Remember that the cranberries will add inter-galactic punch. Choose a mould with height, like Old St Paul's Church spire – think skywards and beyond! When the jelly mixture is melted, strained and ready, pour 100 ml/3⅓ fl oz/generous ⅓ cup into the mould adding a dash of blue Curaçao to enhance its hue. Let it set for 20 minutes.

Over ice, quickset the rest of the mixture, reserving 40 ml/1½ fl oz/8 tsp to create a final even layer on the jelly base. As it thickens carefully add your coral jelly cubes and gradually spoon into the mould. When full add the reserve 40 ml/1½ fl oz/8 tsp of jelly and place in the refrigerator to set.

CANDIED ROSES

Candied food is always a crowd pleaser. Sam's obsession peaked when he spent 90 quid in a single order at luxury hamper specialists Fortnum and Mason. It included two entire candied pineapples. Making these would be laborious and sticky, involving many successive sugar baths and hours of time. Thankfully our candied roses are super-quick to do, but look just as awesome.

The dish began life as a starter (appetizer) but the sweetness confused everyone. It's a lot more appropriate as a dessert or even as edible table décor. Guests pluck the individual sugar petals nestled within the complete roses.

1.5g gum arabic
1 egg white
rose essence, to taste
4 roses (for consumption)
6 for display
50 g/1³/₄ oz/¹/₄ cup white sugar

Mix the gum arabic with the egg white and add a couple of drops of rose essence to boost the flavour. The gum arabic must be thoroughly mixed in. We use the tines of fork to do this; probably not the most effective tool but it's a habit now.

Pluck all the petals of the roses for eating. Discard any that aren't absolutely perfect. Using your thumbs as spatulas, delicately coat the petal with a fine layer of the egg white mixture on both sides. Too much of the mixture and the sugar will go soggy when you put it on.

Now sprinkle the sugar across the petal using a teaspoon and set aside in a dry place to dry. This can be done a day ahead of service and you'll need a minimum of 40 minutes drying time.

Carefully insert the sugar-coated petals into the complete roses and place in a vase for service.

LANVIN MERINGUES

There was a dark moment when *AnOther* magazine asked us to make a cake designed by Lanvin. It had to be big enough so someone could jump out of it before the whole lot exploded. This presents problems in terms of structure, scale of endeavour and stability of ingredients. We realized we'd need a recipe that was simple to make and would last out on display for a couple weeks before being destroyed in a mesmerizing explosion. Meringues held the key.

The recipe makes enough meringues for 33,000 people and uses a quarter of a tonne (250 kg) of caster (superfine) sugar and the same amount of icing (confectioners') sugar! We like to sex up the meringues by serving them with whipped double (heavy) cream flavoured with liqueur de violet.

MAKES ENOUGH FOR 33,000 PEOPLE
8,333 large egg whites
250,000 g/8818 oz/125 cups caster (superfine) sugar
250,000 g/8818 oz/217 cups icing (confectioners') sugar

IF MAKING FOR 20 USE:
5 large egg whites
150 g/5 oz/$^3/_4$ cup caster sugar
150 g/5 oz/scant 1$^1/_3$ cups icing sugar

Preheat the oven 110°C/225°F/Gas Mark $^1/_4$ and line two baking sheets with parchment paper.

Beat the whites to stiff peak at a medium speed before racking up the speed and adding the caster (superfine) sugar, a spoonful at a time. If you add the sugar slowly (3–4 second-intervals) your meringue will be triumphant but beware not to overbeat.

Sift and fold the icing (confectioners') sugar into the mixture, a third at a time, using a spoon or spatula. Don't overbeat. When the mixture is smooth and billowy you are ready to bake.

Portion onto your parchment-lined baking sheets using a pair of spoons and bake for around 1 $^1/_4$ hours. Cool on a wire rack. We like to serve our Lanvin meringues with double (heavy) cream whipped with caster sugar and liqueur de violet to taste, but you can serve however you like.

The Lanvin meringues will keep for a couple weeks. For ideas on explosions have a look at pp.36-43 and take care with any chemicals!

TARTE TATIN

Ancient monks prove that apples are a satanic fruit by carefully dissecting them for their audience. Sliced along the horizontal plane the apple, *Malus pumila*, reveals a pentagram in the arrangement of the endocarp and seeds. Chopped in the vertical plane the monks (slightly worryingly) conflate the endocarp with female sex organs. Make your own mind up as you cook this tasty recipe.

Certainly throughout history apples have been seen as symbols of lascivious and licentious behaviour, forbidden knowledge, temptation, the fall of man, immortality and sin – all to be encouraged at the end of a proper feast.

SERVES 8

6 Granny Smith apples
500 g/1 lb 2 oz puff pastry
100 g/3½ oz/7 tbsp butter, cut into cubes
100 g/3½ oz/½ cup caster (superfine) sugar
icing (confectioners') sugar, for dusting

Preheat the oven to 220°C/425°F/Gas Mark 7.

Peel and core the apples and cut each into 8 segments. Leave out to dry and turn a little brown for a few hours.

Roll out the pastry and cut out a circle that is a little larger than the pan.

Find an ovenproof saucepan about 25 cm/10 in in diameter. Place it on a medium heat and add the butter and sugar. Cook until a caramel starts to form then throw in the apples and continue to cook for a couple of minutes.

Place the pastry on top of the pan and carefully fold in the edges. It's best not to use your fingers unless you want to burn them. Pierce the pastry a few times with a knife to allow the steam to escape. Place the pan in the oven and cook for about 30 minutes, or until the pastry is cooked all the way through.

Remove the pan from the oven and allow it to cool for 5 minutes. With your arm wrapped in a tea (dish) towel, tip the tart onto a serving plate and dust with icing (confectioners') sugar to serve.

BOUDOIR BISCUITS

Boudoir biscuits or ladyfingers are an important component for many of the best desserts, like trifle and tiramisu. We like to make ours from scratch but you can pick up a workhorse version from most supermarkets. Don't be ashamed of this – we do it too when food prep time runs out.

Serve them alongside the jelly or ice cream recipes from this chapter or as an element for your savage and furious trifle (see p.114). Ladyfingers are so good that they were recognized as an "official biscuit" to the court of Savoy. Enjoy!

MAKES ABOUT 30
4 eggs
25 g/1 oz/$\frac{1}{8}$ cup granulated sugar
$\frac{1}{2}$ tsp vanilla extract
$\frac{1}{8}$ tsp cream of tartar
40 g/1$\frac{1}{2}$ oz/scant $\frac{1}{4}$ cup granulated white sugar
65 g/2$\frac{1}{2}$ oz/scant $\frac{1}{2}$ cup flour
icing (confectioners') sugar, for dusting

Preheat the oven to 180°C/350°F/Gas Mark 4.

Divide the eggs into yolks and whites. Place the yolks in the bowl of a mixer and add the 25 g/1 oz/$\frac{1}{8}$ cup of granulated sugar. Beat until the mixture is pale, about 5 minutes. Near the end of the process add the vanilla extract.

Meanwhile, whisk the egg whites and add the cream of tartar. Gradually whisk in the 40 g/1$\frac{1}{2}$ oz/scant $\frac{1}{2}$ cup sugar.

Mix the flour and egg whites into the egg yolk mixture to form a batter. Don't overmix. Spoon the batter into a piping (pastry) bag fitted with a 1-cm/$\frac{1}{2}$-in round nozzle (tip). Have ready a couple of baking sheets lined with parchment paper. Pipe lines of the batter, about 6 cm/2$\frac{1}{2}$ in long, onto the parchment paper. Be sure to leave a 3-cm/1$\frac{1}{4}$-in gap between each, as the mixture will expand as it cooks.

Cook the biscuits for 8 minutes until just starting to brown. Remove to a wire rack to cool and then sprinkle with icing (confectioners') sugar.

AFTER DINNER

OXYGEN AS A COFFEE ALTERNATIVE

Enriched and enhanced atmospheres are no new concept. In the early twentieth century the London Underground was ventilated with ozone to keep the air in the tunnel fresh and bacteria free – a less sinister alternative to the hideous chemical clouds of mustard gas, phosgene and chlorine floating across the continent throughout WWI.

Over the last few years, we at Bompas & Parr have worked hard to look at how airborne ingredients, nutrients and intoxicants can add an extra dimension to a meal or event. This moves far beyond the futurist use of perfumes to offset a dish, evoke a memory or cover up noxious cooking smells coming from the kitchen. If you can get enough of your chosen ingredient into the air as a gas or cloud you can have a real physiological effect on people with every breath they take.

The respiratory scientists at CASE (the Centre for Altitude, Space and Extreme Environment Medicine) helped us with the *Ziggurat of Flavour* where people contribute to their "five a day" through their lungs and eyeballs. By creating a dense fruit-based cloud people could reach recommended vitamin C levels by absorbing it through their body's mucus membranes. Health and safety was a delicate and complex challenge. Using the juice from the wrong fruit or treating it inappropriately could have formed a dangerous chemical cloud. Pineapples contain the flesh eating enzyme bromelian, which, if not denatured before making the cloud, would have started to digest peoples' lungs.

We created an even more successful cloud for Alcoholic Architecture. You entered a gin and tonic mist so dense that it was impossible to see your friend 1 m/3 ft away – there was so much booze in the air between you. Within 15 minutes you could feel the intoxicating effects. The alcohol went straight into the bloodstream bypassing the liver for immediate effect. Scientists were our mixologists calculating the ratio of gin to tonic to ensure everyone was safe. As we were using overproof gin, an inorganic chemist tested the mixture to ensure the whole installation wasn't going to explode if someone lit a cigarette. By spatializing the flavour and creating a super-humid environment you were able to taste the botanicals in the gin much better than you would otherwise.

Recklessly, on the final night we ran neat spirits through the cloud machinery for the Bompas & Parr home team. The crew ended up scattered across London, from King's Cross to Heathrow and Bromley at 5am with no recollection of how we got there. The mystery deepened as we all escaped a hangover.

Assembling the mechanism to generate clouds is probably a bit involved for regular feasting. It will also leave your front room damp and sticky. With a little planning it's still possible, though, to end the feast with a turbo-charged and enhanced atmosphere.

We keep a 72-kg/159-lb compressed oxygen cylinder handy to sober up carousers and sots at the end of a meal. It was pretty easy to get hold of and uses food grade oxygen (see Suppliers). The BBC has documented how oxygen enriched atmospheres have been used by casinos to make people feel more alert. You can use it as a bracing and showy alternative to coffee.

Guests will be amazed and surprised as you heft the mighty oxygen canister into the dining room. At 72 kg/159 lb and awkwardly shaped it's a two man struggle but this adds to the glory of the result. Screw it on full blast giving guests a tornado of chilled oxygen in the face. If your canister is similarly filled to 230 bars, the oxygen will come out with force enough to rip paintings from the wall and knock over glasses.

Notes on procedure
Extinguish any candles or naked flames of course.

Try to minimize air change in the room before blasting the oxygen. The less draught there is, the greater the impact, so shut doors and windows. Also, the greater the level of oxygen in the room, the larger the effect – smaller spaces work better.

CIGARETTE COURSE

Neither of us smoke but we've noticed how compelling a simple pineapple studded with cigarettes can be. At the end of a meal personal strictures are loosened. Legally approved addictive drugs provide just enough danger. Cigarettes have éclat from years of glamour advertising.

Snuff would also be appropriate at the end of a feast. Be sure to secure an appropriately grand snuff mull. We once hired a horse hoof cigarette holder and ram's horn snuff mull to round off a meal in Brighton. Surprisingly a full 90 per cent of diners tucked in, despite only 30 per cent being habitual tobacco users. People like something to regret the next day - a smoke isn't as bad as a pregnancy.

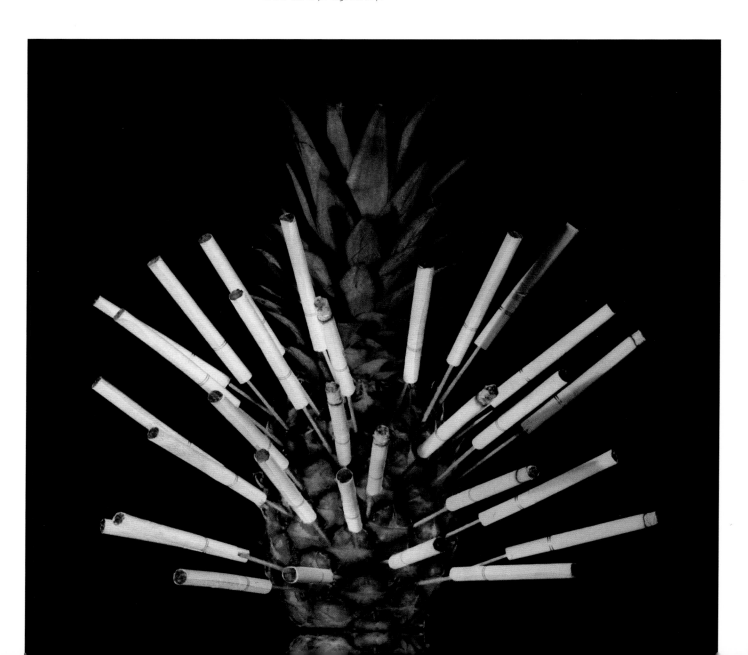

CHEWING GUM

Michelin-starred chefs and McDonald's both set out to give customers the ultimate food experience for their money. They'll use any means necessary to do so. This is particularly true of molecular gastronomers who like tinkering with textures.

The same industrial ingredients are now being used in Michelin-starred restaurants as well as mass-market joints, sometimes with awesome effect. Take for example transglutaminase which chefs call "meat glue". It bonds together the proteins in different bits of meat, sticking them together. Chef Heston Blumenthal uses it to conjure dishes like Ballotine of Anjou Pigeon and Chef Wylie Dufresne makes a powerful case for it in the awesome *Momofuku Cookbook*. But transglutaminase is also employed to make horrors such as the meat chessboard of light and dark meat. Good taste must be exercised. McDonald's uses it to meld the perfect nugget shape.

Methyl cellulose is perhaps even more interesting. It's used in haute cuisine as a thickener and has the unique property of setting when hot and melting when cold. It's also used to make hot non-leak pie filler in chain restaurants, as a sexual lubricant, laxative, slime in films such as *Ghostbusters* and as the jizz in pornos. Fun stuff!

The cross-pollination of ingredients and creativity between the world's best chefs and industrial ingredients and chemicals prompted us see how far we could go. What's the ultimate industrial food ingredient?

The answer is gum base – technically described as non-nutritative, non-digestible masticatory product. It's a plastic with zero nutritional value and the key ingredient in chewing gum, a food you don't swallow. That said, gum sales were £250 million in the UK last year and if you walk into a room 25 per cent of the people in it will have a packet in their handbag or pocket.

We've obsessed about gum base for the last three years. The minimum order from manufacturers across the globe is a quarter of a tonne. We were stumped until Lucy Clark of the Marks & Spencer confectionery team had Swiss manufacturers send us some. It is a magical material, readily absorbing and releasing flavour (alongside lots of sugar). Children can make complex flavours like smoke and white truffle totally unsupervised.

(recipe continues overleaf)

The idea behind the *Artisanal Chewing Gum Factory* at Whiteleys Shopping Centre, London, was to give everyone a chance to get messy with gum base and create potentially classy flavoured gum on a micro-scale. We managed to track down 200 flavours ranging from yuzu and Lahara fruit to gin and tonic. This gave us 40,000 different possibilities. Flavour expert Niki Segnit even came up with a passion fruit and foie gras combo that changed flavour as you chewed. You can create your own fancy gum following this recipe. Provided you can get hold of the gum base!

Melt together as much gum base, glucose and glycerine at the ratios above and then separate into 15 g/^{1}/$_2$ oz portions each in its own plastic (microwavable bowl). These are then ready for action whenever you need to make gum:

CHEWING GUM RECIPE (MAKES 10 PIECES)

10 g gum base
6 g glucose
1 g glycerine
0.5 ml flavouring
1.5 ml citric acid
2 drops of food colouring
18 g/2^1/$_4$ tbsp icing (confectioners') sugar, plus extra for sprinkling

EQUIPMENT

Microwavable bowl
Mixing spoon
Pipette
Knife

Take a bowl and combine 15 g/^{1}/$_2$ oz of combined gum base, glucose and glycerine. Heat in the microwave for 2 minutes and stir.

Add the flavouring, water, citric acid and food colouring to the hot mixture and stir again.

Add half of the icing (confectioners') sugar into the bowl and knead until mixed, then add the remaining icing sugar to the mixture.

Sprinkle some icing sugar onto the table and roll the mixture into a long sausage. Portion and package.

SHERBET & PILLS

As a child realizing that the secret to unlimited sherbet was simply mixing bicarbonate of soda (baking soda) and citric acid with icing (confectioners') sugar was like discovering the philosopher's stone. Mountains of sherbet are probably the cheapest and most joyful thing to make for feasting and the reaction between the acid and alkaline in the presence of salivial moisture is alchemically brilliant.

When we started making sherbets at Bompas & Parr we didn't know where to bulk order citric acid but found we could get if for free from the chemist. A government sponsored scheme means that if you ask nicely they give you a pack with syringes, needles, a condom and citric acid, which is used to mix with brown heroin to form a citrate salt so it's suitable for injecting. For a while we were making so much sherbet that one of the interns' daily jobs was to hit up all the London chemists for citric acid. They came from good families so eyebrows were raised. Of course none of the chemists believed the "sherbet" story and thought something far more sinister was going on.

Eventually we wanted to raise our sherbet game and bought a beast of a pill press from China. The heavy-duty stamp compresses sherbet into hard candies. The guys running the import company have to report each pill press they sell to the police and won't let you buy pill forms with car logos, smiley faces or doves on.

700 g/1 lb 9 oz/6 cups icing (confectioners') sugar
300 g/10½ oz citric acid
100 g/3½ oz/½ cup bicarbonate of soda (baking soda)

Sift the icing (confectioners') sugar into a bowl and add the citric acid and bicarbonate of soda (baking soda). Scale the recipe to make mountains of the stuff (we use 25 kg/55 lb bags of icing sugar to get started).

Store in an airtight container for use whenever you need it.

SUGAR SCULPTURE

The Renaissance saw a seriously important introduction to European cuisine, an essential addition that now completes any proper banquet - sugar. Indeed, in the sixteenth and seventeenth centuries the word "banquet" actually meant the final sweet course of a feast. It was so special that diners were often required to relocate to the garden or a purpose-built venue, one befitting of such a splendid new course.

The banquet was typically more lighthearted than the other courses, music would be played and visitors encouraged to dance around. Servants weren't present so the banquet was a place for indiscretions, the gateway to romance. Aside from the mountains of tarts, pies, cakes and fruit, sugar sculptures would also be displayed. These sculptures linked the art of the sculptor with that of the cook. The humanist Filippo Beroaldo reported that the 1487 wedding of Lucrezia d'Este and Giovanni Bentivoglio in Bologna, Italy, featured giant sugar sculptures of castles, ships, people and animals, and a flaming wheel of fireworks that accidentally ignited some of the wedding guests. At the wedding feast of Maria de' Medici to Henri IV in Florence in 1600, the groom was absent, but his image appeared on the table in the form of an impressive equestrian statue, modelled in sugar by sculptor Pietro Tacca.

You can create your own using sugar sculptures using this pastillage recipe. The first step is to create a mould. We make a traditional walnut mould using food grade silicone. Buy some - you can mould anything and it comes with better instructions then we can give you.

FOR THE PASTILLAGE
25 g/1 oz gum tragacanth
450 g/1 lb/4 cups icing (confectioners') sugar, plus extra for dusting
60 ml/2 fl oz/¼ cup water

Sift together the gum tragacanth and the icing (confectioners') sugar. Incrementally mix in the water, kneading the pastillage between your fingers until it feels like dough. While you work the pastillage keep the rest wrapped in cling film (plastic wrap) or in a bowl covered with a damp cloth. Otherwise it dries out.

Work the right amount of pastillage into a mould well dusted with icing sugar. Remove any excess with a sharp flat-edged knife. Carefully remove the pastillage from the mould and leave it to dry.

If done correctly this will keep unrefrigerated for 100 years. The secret to sugar sculpture is yours. For a brown pastillage, mix in ground cinnamon until the colour pleases.

- CHEAPER VERSION -

If this is too time consuming/complex we've got another technique. Go to a car boot sale or rubbish antiques dealer and buy cheap porcelain figures. The sort of thing you probably threw out in shame when your grandmother died. Seaside towns are goldmines for mint condition porcelain tat of this sort.

We are obsessed with porcelain. The recipe to make it was once the most highly prized secret of European courts and the name porcelain has a wonderfully smutty origin. It's derived from the Italian term for cowry shell *porcellana* as it shares qualities of lightness, value and a shiny hard surface. The lewd bit is that *porcellana* translates as "little pig" - when you flip the cowry over the underside looks like a pig's vulva. Bear this etymological curiosity in mind next time you are sipping tea from a fine porcelain cup.

Give your porcelain treasures an undercoat using a saccharine pastel coloured spray paint. We match our pantones to Fox's party rings.

Using air tools, spray successive layers of sugar icing of your chosen shade. You need to thin your icing (icing sugar + water) using water so that it can be blasted through the air tool (we use a tool normally used to spray paint cars).

As the successive layers build up tiny sugar crystals will form. No one will understand how you've achieved the results.

- SUPER EASY VERSION -

Make sugar sculptures by making a concentrated sugar solution (as much sugar as you can get to dissolve in boiling water) and placing any object you like in it. Over time crystals will form on the surface encasing it in a beautiful crystalline structure. The rougher the crystal growing surface the better they will form so something like lace will work well.

When growing crystals like this we think about J.G. Ballard's *The Crystal World* where a West African jungle experiences an apocalyptic phenomenon that crystallizes everything it touches. Trees are metamorphosed into enormous jewels, pythons blinded with gemstone eyes rear in heraldic poses and crocodiles encased in second glittering skin lurch down the river. As lepers set off into the ossifying jungle to find paradise, slowly the crystals grow.

COCKTAILS

MILKSHAKE ALEXANDRA

"I LIKE THE EFFECT DRINK HAS ON ME, SO WHAT'S
THE POINT OF STAYING SOBER?"
- OLIVER REED -

McDonald's meals are almost perfect in terms of giving your body what it craves. The carefully calibrated combination of fat, salt and sugar makes the food deeply compelling. The flavours are paired in with furious marketing and thrilling fast-food environments, all geared to stimulate your neurons. These are the cells that trigger the brain's reward system and release dopamine, the chemical that motivates our behaviour, and makes us want to eat more. The same receptors are targeted by powerful amphetamines.

Professor Kessler, ex-commissioner of the US Food and Drug Administration (FDA) explains it well: "Many of us have what's called a 'bliss point', at which we derive the greatest pleasure from sugar, fat or salt. Combined in the right way, they make a product indulgent, near irresistible and high in hedonic value." McDonald's gets this pretty much spot on. In terms of "hedonic value" you can't get more for your money.

Only two things are missing from the ultimate "happy meal" - proper tablecloths and booze. If you combine these elements with your usual burger-based meal it'll be unforgettable. It's not too hard to do with some forward planning. At Bompas & Parr we sometimes like to take white tablecloths, napkins and silver candelabra when visiting Maccy D's. You get strange looks but it's worth it in terms of the frisson of danger. We also like to take a bottle of Courvoisier XO to add to our milkshakes. It's a bit crass but hugely rewarding for the level of depth and complexity it adds to the shake. Give it a blast.

SERVES 1
1 medium vanilla milkshake
1 heavy slug of Courvoisier XO

Drink the milkshake down a bit to make room for the booze. Slip in a heavy slug of Courvoisier XO when the McDonald's branch manager isn't looking. Give it a stir with your red, yellow and white straw and enjoy.

As a bonus, grate some fresh black truffles onto your nuggets.

KHAT COCKTAIL

SERVES 1

50 ml/1¾ fl oz/scant ¼
cup dark rum
25 ml/1 fl oz/2 tbsp lime juice
25 ml/1 fl oz/2 tbsp pineapple juice
25 ml/1 fl oz/2 tbsp orange juice
1 tsp maple syrup
1 dash of khat bitters (see below)
3 sprigs of khat, to decorate

FOR THE KHAT BITTERS

1 banana leaf wrap of khat
200 ml/7 fl oz/generous ¾ cup
flavourless spirit, such as vodka

This cocktail has a strong penetrating odour, and is composed of spirits that make it sweetish, hot, burning and pungent to the palate. The inclusion of khat means that even experienced "alcoholists" will appreciate what they are dicing with.

We came up with the cocktail when asked to create something for the late night opening of The Museum of London's pirate exhibition. The museum has a full-sized reconstruction of the dark winding streets of Victorian Wapping complete with a wild animal emporium, ale house, sailor's lodgings and corner that smells like piss. For the evening we took over the alehouse and wanted to make cocktails that explored the gustatory and moral implications of piracy combining the preferred drugs of historical pirates – booze, with those of modern Somali pirates – khat.

Khat is an East African plant that stimulates like amphetamines. It's not illegal in the UK, but jolly hard to find. With only a day to track it down we tore through Somali shops across the capital taking in Brixton, Peckham, Harlesden and Paddington. Asking for khat we were mainly directed to pet shops but we finally ran it to ground in Finsbury Park. The khat comes delicately wrapped in banana leaves and is airlifted to London to be consumed fresh. It has a punchy green flavour, like eating a fresh plucked bay leaf.

We turned the khat into a homemade bitters that finish the cocktails, further garnishing with enough khat to give museum-goers a powerful hit. It made for an exciting museum experience. You rarely have to warn people with heart conditions away from the cocktails.

Shake the ingredients with ice and serve decorated with the bonus khat.

For the khat bitters

Put a handful of khat into a 1 litre/1¾ pint/4 cup cream whipper with the flavourless spirit. Charge the whipper with nitrous oxide and leave for 30 seconds before carefully releasing the pressure. This will almost instantly infuse the spirit with the pungent flavour of khat.

If you don't have a cream whipper, leave the khat to infuse in the spirit for two days before straining it out. The former method is preferred as the active ingredients in khat break down over time. The sooner you get to infuse the spirit the better. The khat bitters will keep for a week in the refrigerator.

FAST AND EFFECTIVE DRINKS FOR BEFORE AND AFTER THE FEAST

Over the last few years there's been a global cocktail renaissance. Drinks being served include ever more exotic ingredients and are made to increasingly complex formulas. If you go to fancy bars it is now possible to buy cocktails aged in oak casks, chilled with hand carved ice and fixed with spirits sourced from shipwrecks.

Making a fine mixed drink for your guests doesn't need to be this tricky. You don't need to be a cocktail bore and waste time with fussy formulas and elaborate preparations. These four drinks sidestep silliness and aim to put something excellent inside a glass. After all, drinking is for joy and pleasure. Behold!

Note: All these cocktails are easily scalable, so the recipes are given in parts. This will let you eyeball making large batches in jugs (pitchers) or individual drinks as the need arises. Trust your own palate and balance to taste.

- FOR BEFORE DINNER -

VENEZIANO

1 part Campari
1 part red vermouth
6 parts white wine

Stir in a highball or wine glass over ice. You can add a twist of orange peel to jazz it up if you like.

WHITE PORT AND INDIAN TONIC

1 part white port
3 parts Indian tonic

Build over ice in a tall glass and decorate with a half wheel of lime.

Note: We've noticed that people with a sweet tooth like a dash of sugar syrup in their drink, while seasoned drinkers can handle a lower tonic to port ratio in this one.

FLOC DE GASCOGNE

1 part sweet white wine (chilled)
1 part Armagnac
single cube of ice

Build in a very small glass, stir and drop in the single cube of ice. Good with cheese.

B & P

3 parts Cognac
1 part ruby port

Place the ingredients in a rocks glass and stir for a couple of seconds. Serve immediately.

ALCHEMICAL MOUNTAIN BREW

- BOTTLED COCKTAIL -

SERVES 11-12

THE DAY BEFORE BOTTLING FOR THE PINEAPPLE SYRUP

500 ml/17 fl oz/generous 2 cups water

500 g/1 lb 2 oz/2 ½ cups granulated sugar

1 pineapple

FOR THE COCKTAILS

120 ml/4 fl oz/½ cup rich pineapple syrup

30 ml/1 fl oz/2 tbsp green chartreuse

1 litre/1¾ pints/4 cups Hendrick's gin

1 litre/1#/4 pints/4 cups weak green tea

1 litre/1¾ pints/4 cups seltzer

200 ml/7 fl oz/generous ¾ cup lemon juice

5 drops fluorescein (optional)

edible flowers, to decorate (optional)

FOR THE PARAPHENALIA

300 ml/10 fl oz/1 ¼ cups glass bottles

bottle caps

bottle capper

This bottled cocktail is deceptively refreshing and punishingly strong. Bottling is optional but it gives the fluids time to intermingle and if done the day before frees you from mixing fine drinks in the thick of the action.

We came up with the cocktail for a dinner in the Masonic Temple at Andaz Hotel, London, alongside a screening of Alejandro Jodorowsky's cult film *Holy Mountain*. The movie includes tarot, alchemists, limbless dwarves, castration, a cemetery party and frogs dressed as Mayan princes - to measure up, the food and drinks had to be epic.

We worked with chef Martin Scholz on a menu so savage it combined veal, bone marrow, snails and black pudding (blood sausage) in a single dish. The meal culminated with the procession of a 1-m (3-ft) ice phallus - only slightly legitimized by a similar scene in the film. The giant ice cock ended up being hacked apart with an ice axe and the shards used to chill cocktails.

We wanted this drink to glow the lurid colour of Mountain Dew while still tasting outstanding. The key was adding an infinitesimal amount of fluorescein, known as Yellow No 7 in the US and C14350 in the EU. The dye is used regularly to dye the entire Chicago River green on St Patrick's Day and in laser eye surgery, but when used in drinks you need to be sparing. You only need a tiny bit for a haunting glow and too much can give people a heart attack!

If you don't want to walk the line of danger leave the fluorescein out, or colour up with another dye.

The day before bottling

Make the pineapple syrup by bringing the water to the boil in a pan and stirring in the sugar. Keep stirring until all the sugar is dissolved. Now dice the flesh of the pineapple (discarding the core, skin and such) into 1-cm/½ -in cubes and leave to steep in the syrup for 24 hours. Strain out the pineapple chunks and you're good to go. This gives you more syrup than you will need for this particular cocktail but leftovers keep for a week (covered in the refrigerator) are handy to have around.

Making the cocktails

Combine the strained pineapple syrup, green chartreuse, Hendrick's gin, weak green tea, seltzer, lemon juice and potentially the fluorescein in a large bowl. Balance the acidity and sugar of the drink with either more lemon juice or pineapple syrup. Funnel into sterilized and polished bottles, and finally cap the bottles.

To serve

An hour before serving the cocktails chill them by putting them in a bucket (or bathtub) filled with ice. Uncap and you're away.

If you aren't bottling them, then serve the cocktail in a highball glass over ice and decorate with an edible flower (nasturtiums are good, if ruinously expensive).

Masterstroke

Design and print your own labels for the bottle. When we serve the Alchemical Mountain Brew we use occult labels printed in black and gold.

YELLOW FEVER PUNCH

- HOT PUNCH -

Yellow Fever Punch pisses on mulled wine and is a compelling argument for cold weather. The mixture tastes like it actually might be good for your health. A hot toddy turbo-charged with extra spices and Kamm & Sons ginseng spirit. For 5,000 years the Chinese have turned to ginseng to ward off infection, increase libido and improve memory. Importantly for drinkers, ginseng can also repair liver damage and help process alcohol from the bloodstream! I should coco. Don't be deceived by this - the punch is so fragrant it's hard to distinguish the entire bottle of Scotch that's gone into it. Over-enthusiastic prescription will leave you worse off tomorrow.

Serves 8-10 people, depending on how thirsty they are and how cold it is outside!

SERVES 8-10

1 bottle of Scotch

300 ml/10 fl oz/1 1/4 cups ginger ale

200 ml/7 fl oz/generous 3/4 cup water

200 ml/7 fl oz/generous 3/4 cup Kamm & Sons ginseng spirit

50 g/1 3/4 oz/1/4 cup demerera (raw brown) sugar (or caster/superfine or brown... whatever you have)

25 g/1 oz/generous 1/8 cup raisins

1 fresh pineapple, peeled, cored and cut into dice

zest of 1 orange

zest of 1 lemon

juice of 1/2 lemon

2 cinnamon sticks

1 star anise

1/2 freshly grated nutmeg

3 granules of instant coffee (for bitters)

Put all the ingredients into a pot and cook gently, making sure that it never comes to the boil. You'll need to adjust the balance of flavours as you go - the punch changes considerably as you cook it.

To serve

When ready to serve the hot beverage, adjust with sweetness (sugar) or acidity (lemon juice). Serve warm in a teacup with a saucer and make sure you dole out the alcoholic pineapple chunks too. They're explosively boozy.

Less seasoned guests may find the recipe too strong. Balance it up with more hot water and sugar.

FRUIT SALAD OF DEATH

This green gin punch is absurdly potent and inspired by performance hula-hooper, Marawa the Amazing. She performs the Fruit Salad of Death. You can drink it... with care.

We first served this drink for a meal inspired by sex, death, horror and magic and wanted something that grabbed you by the throat. The punch is so full on we had to use tiny 35 ml/1¼ fl oz glasses. People thought it contained amphetamines.

SERVES 50 OR MORE

2 pineapples, peeled, cored and cut into dice
3 oranges, cut into half wheels
3 lemons, cut into half wheels
3 limes, cut into wheels
3 bottles of gin
600 ml/1 pint/2½ cups sugar syrup (p.122)
300 ml/10 fl oz/1¼ cups lemon juice
200 ml/7 fl oz/generous ¾ cup liqueur de violet
2 punnets (cartons) of raspberries
3 bottles of Champagne
liquid nitrogen or plenty of ice cubes, for chilling

Put the pineapples and citrus fruit into a punchbowl and add the gin, sugar syrup, lemon juice and liqueur de violet. Refrigerate for 3 hours to chill and let the juices intermingle.

When ready for grand service empty in the raspberries and champagne and keep chilled by constantly adding liquid nitrogen from a handy thermos flask.

If you don't have liquid nitrogen then ladle the concoction over ice cubes for service.

If you want a longer serve then use three bottles of soda water and add at the same time as the Champagne.

EAGLE TAIL

**SYRUP OF ETHER
(ENOUGH FOR 8 DRINKS)**
75 ml/2½ fl oz/5 tbsp sugar syrup
5 ml/1 tsp ether
Mix the ether with the standard
sugar syrup (see p.122 for recipe)
and store in a well-capped glass
bottle. This will keep refrigerated
for a week.

SERVES 1
35 ml/1¼ fl oz/heaping 2
tbsp aged brandy
35 ml/1¼ fl oz/heaping 2 tbsp old
kirsch
5 ml/1 tsp absinthe
5 ml/1 tsp syrup of ether
1 maraschino cherry, to decorate

Drinking this cocktail is an initiation ceremony in its own right. It was developed by Aleister Crowley (1875–1947) the occultist, mystic and astrologer whose sexually deviant ceremonial magic titillated the early twentieth century. Crowley's mother referred to him as "the Beast" a term he revelled in and he founded the religious philosophy of Thelema. The supreme moral law being: "Do what thou wilt".

The philosophy of Thelema and Crowley's personal life were dogged by scandal, outrage and sensation – the esoteric practices being confused with devil worship. But even with rumours of women having sex with goats at Crowley's Abbey of Thelema he was voted the seventy-third greatest Briton of all time in a poll by the BBC in 2002.

Crowley's less notorious pastimes included chess, mountaineering and cocktails. In 1902 he led the first European party to attempt K2 but was forced to turn back at 6096 m/20,000 ft. The cocktails are more successful despite the inclusion of outrageous ingredients. His Kubla Khan No 2 is a dry Martini laced with laudanum and one cocktail even contains small quantities of strychnine sulphate (rat poison so probably best avoided).

We were first introduced to the drinks of "The Great Beast" by mixologist Stuart Bale who had tracked down the recipes but was lacking the exotic ingredients. We were able to furnish ether for the magnificent Eagle Tail – a cocktail that tastes like black forest gateau with a gunning chainsaw finish.

Ether is not too hard to track down (for a full discussion of ether see our previous book *Cocktails with Bompas & Parr*). We were happy to discover the drink as Crowley's formula solves the major problems of ether's extreme volatility by incorporating it into a sugar syrup. In the past we'd had to impregnate soft fruits with the ether to stop the chemical evaporating before you could ingest it.

Shake over ice and serve in a Martini glass decorated with a maraschino cherry. It's such a strong drink you could safely split it between even two committed drinkers and serve in peculiarly small glasses.

If you can't get hold of ether, or the cocktail strikes you as dangerous and depraved, you might try another of Crowley's gayer concoctions. Soak raspberries overnight in Grand Marnier and float them in pink champagne to serve.

COCKTAIL OF THE FUTURE

"WE SHALL ESCAPE THE ABSURDITY OF GROWING A WHOLE
CHICKEN IN ORDER TO EAT THE BREAST OR WING BY GROWING
THESE PARTS SEPARATELY UNDER A SUITABLE MEDIUM."
– WINSTON CHURCHILL –

Across the twenteith century weapons technologists, secretive government agencies, combat futurologists and warmongers have scanned the pages of science fiction looking for insight into future battlefields and the inspiration for powerful combat technologies.

The last decade has seen the development of weaponized cyborg insects, combat exoskeletons and practical battlefield lasers – concepts once confined to the pages of twentieth century science fiction.

We were inspired to go on our own space odyssey and conquer dishes featured in science fiction (SF). "Food plays a significant role in genre as one of the clearest measures of how far we have journeyed from the present." (J.P. Retzinger, 2008) As such many SF authors and film directors invest considerable energy imagining the food of the future and their predictions offer areas for culinary speculation and innovation.

Being able to create the terrifying milk-based intoxicants from *A Clockwork Orange*, low gravity food, nacho bananas (*The 6th Day*), ethically dubious transgenic meat inspired by the pulsating flesh tumour of *The Space Merchants* or entire meals in a pill (*Conquest of Space*) may not delineate the future, but at the very least it can provoke conversations around how we will eating in centuries to come.

This is important as the future is not set and by talking about it and trying things out, you can help shape it. Black & Decker may not yet market a re-hydrator that turns 3-in Pizza Hut pizzas into cheesy 16 in, ready to eat in 3 seconds (*Back to the Future II*), but practically exploring the concept may goad food technologists to work up a prototype.

Scientist Gregory Benford writes that: "Science has often followed cultural anticipation, not led it." (2007). After all journeys to the moon were depicted in Georges Méliès, *Le Voyage Dans la Lune* 67 years before Neil Armstrong set foot upon it. The astronaut even inscribed a copy of science fiction author and

(recipe continues overleaf)

futurologist Arthur C. Clark's monograph *Wingless on Luna* with: "To Arthur, who visualized the nuances of lunar flying long before I experienced them!"

So looking at SF as a source for creativity we were able to imagine the future, think of the ethical implications of new food ways (eating reprocessed human protein in *Solyent Green*), play with possible benefits, explore avoidable tragedies and ultimately engage in a deeper conversation about science, food, technology and our future.

Some of our forays were successful, others opened a Pandora's box of shame and sore heads. None more so than reverse engineering the recipe for Douglas Adam's notorious Pan Galactic Gargle Blaster a fictional cocktail from *The Hitchhiker's Guide to the Galaxy*. The drink is so potent it's described as the "alcoholic equivalent of a mugging" with an effect of "having your brain smashed out by a slice of lemon wrapped round a large gold brick." Check out the book for the original formula.

While we might not have had Douglas Adams' Fallan marsh gas or Arcturan Mega-gin, we did have a few tricks up our sleeve to help make the most intoxicating drink in the world.

SERVES 1
20 ml/4 tsp overproof vodka
20 ml/4 tsp overproof gin
10 ml/2 tsp crème de menthe
80 mg caffeine
carbonate with 2 charges nitrous oxide
Champagne, to top

Mix the vodka, gin and crème de menthe and stir in the carefully weighted caffeine. Place the concoction in a cream whipper and charge twice with nitrous oxide (hippy crack). Now place the mixture at the bottom of a champagne flute and top with Champagne.

Now you have made the world's first carbonated and caffeinated overproof cocktail – arguably the world's most intoxicating drink. "Carbonation dramatically increases the rate of alcohol absorption" (Roberts and Robertson, 2007) as the alcohol can bypass your liver being absorbed directly through the lung. The nitrous oxide and caffeine have effects all of their own – a drink to be respected. *The Hitchhiker's Guide to the Galaxy* also implies that there are multiple voluntary organizations available to rehabilitate those who would try the Pan Galactic Gargle Blaster.

Why not have a go at tracking down your own science fiction foods and prototyping them? If they are as punchy as this your feast will get off to a roaring start.

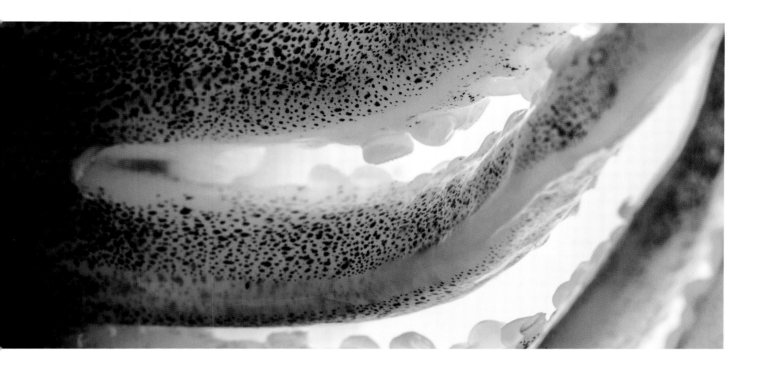

TENTACLE MARTINI

SERVES 1
60 ml/2 fl oz/¼ cup gin
10 ml/2 tsp green chartreuse
1 tentacle
(therefore 1 octopus is enough for
8 drinks!)

This is the best and worst of cocktails. It's simple to prepare for the feast, and has the dash and swagger of drinks from the golden age of cocktails with all the novelty of a Tiki concoction. Beware that, in common with all Martinis, it's best suited to alcoholics – a real swashbuckler.

It came about when we only had gin, green chartreuse and a few octopus in the refrigerator. Working with what you've got is one of the great joys of cocktailing. Every so often you stumble on a winner that delights your palate a lot more than you think it should.

Sam remembered hearing about Henri Toulouse-Lautrec, the inbred dwarf and artist, hosting a wild party where he served guests 2,000 cocktails including one of gin flamed with port with a sardine in it. It's pretty weird, but the sardine does the job of the olive in the Martini or the onion in the Gibson, the port adding sweetness a bit like vermouth.

The good thing is that there's so much alcohol in there it effectively cooks the fishy tentacle. Good luck getting through three.

Stir the gin and green chartreuse over ice and strain into a frozen Martini glass. Decorate with the tentacle. For extra panache skewer the tentacle with a cocktail sword.

MY LOVE LETTER TO CHAMPAGNE TOWERS BY FIONA LEAHY

Champagne towers; the very sight of one makes my spirits soar. They are the perfect gleaming symmetrical monuments to the good times fragile glass pyramids of decadence.

The romantic in me has such fond notions of the 1920s, a time when champagne was served in coupes (from towers of course) and scarlet lipped ladies with matching scarlet nails and marcel waves clinked glasses.

This love of nostalgia and an appreciation for the bespoke made champagne towers are irresistible to me. The fact that they need to be created, glass by glass in a painstaking fashion, which takes hours to complete, coupled with the fragility, as one wrong move and the whole thing topples over and crashes... The fact that you can't just buy a champagne tower and that they need to be expertly created is what makes them is so compellingly seductive. It is the drinks equivalent to a dinner that takes days to prepare; an antidote to whatever is fast and immediate. The champagne tower is by its very nature a deliberate planned staged attack on the mundane and expected.

I made my first champagne tower for Marilyn Manson and Dita Von Teese's wedding. They have a shared love of nostalgia and once that one was built I was hooked. I most recently "erected" one for my birthday and fiiled it with vintage pink champagne. The pouring of the champagne, the trickling from glass to glass, the goosebumps that it might all go wrong, the sighs and gasps when it doesn't, and then the reward of an almost overflowing glass. As far as I'm concerned a champagne tower is pretty much the guarantee of a great party - it sets the tone. Why serve champagne glasses from a tray when they can be gingerly plucked from a tower full to the brim? It puts performance and spectacle into the art of drinking and it is an art if you want it to be...

01

A solid, firm base for your tower is essential. A separate table is best and a spillage tray at the bottom of the tower or underneath the table is ideal for catching the overflow of champagne.

02

To make a tower you need to use coupe glasses (champagne saucers) not flutes. The key to the tower is symmetry and uniformity so ensure all the glasses are identical in size and proportion.

03

The tower is essentially made up of successively smaller layers of squares. For example, if the bottom layer is made up of 10 glasses by 10 glasses, the layer above that would be 9 by 9, the layer above that would be 8 by 8, and so on.

04

Make sure each glass touches the surrounding glasses. When done correctly you will see a perfect diamond-shaped gap between each glass.

05

When building the next layer, centre the stem of the glass over the diamond openings that were created by the layer below. Carefully fill in the layer with glasses. Slow and steady, this is not a job to be rushed.

06

Repeat this assembly process until there is a single coupe glass on top. Hurrah!

07

Once fully assembled, begin slowly pouring champagne from the top glass and it will trickle downwards. I recommend using jeroboams or magnums of champagne as flow is important and smaller bottles fill fewer glasses.

08

Glasses need to be filled to the brim. This makes the action of delicately sipping from a nearly overflowing glass an act of care and attention. I promise after all this effort a glass of champagne from a tower tastes the most sublime.

THE MORNING AFTER

CHIEFTAIN PANCAKES

These American pancakes are so hairy and muscly you can really gorge on them. A large stack of them will form the basis of a nutritious breakfast. We find that they are a great restorative.

SERVES 8

FOR THE DRY INGREDIENTS
400 g/14 oz/generous 2¾ cups plain (all-purpose) flour
80 g/3 oz/scant ½ cup granulated sugar
2 rounded tsp baking powder
pinch of salt

FOR THE WET INGREDIENTS
4 large eggs
90 g/3¼ oz/scant ½ cup unsalted butter, melted, plus extra for frying
700 ml/1¼ pints/generous 3 cups milk
1 teaspoon vanilla extract

Mix all the dry ingredients together. Beat the wet ingredients together in a separate bowl starting with the eggs. Pour the wet ingredients into the dry ingredients and mix until the flour is well mixed in. Ignore lumps.

Heat a frying pan (skillet) over a high heat until little beads of water run all over the surface. If they skip over the edge your pan is too hot – turn it down. Now melt a little pat (piece) of butter in the pan and smear it round with kitchen paper (paper towels) so the pan is evenly coated. Too much fat in the pan and you'll be frying the pancakes. Carefully pour your mixture into the pan until it reaches a diameter of roughly 10 cm/4 in. When you see little bubbles popping on top of the pancake it's time to flip it over. The other side will take about half the time to be done.

Continue making the pancakes like this until you have a decent stack. Keep adding butter to keep the level of fat in the pan constant – but not too much. If you have extras you can freeze them and cook them in the toaster at a later date for a healthy snack. Sauce with maple syrup or golden syrup.

Bonus suggestion. We add things like IQF fruit (frozen fruit available in most supermarkets) to the batter. You can add whatever you like.

BREAD 'N' BREAKFAST PUDDING

This recipe comes straight from Sam's American mom and it's amazing. It's got all the best bits of a bread and butter pudding but made savoury with the tastiest food going (cheese, bacon, pizza sauce...).

SERVES 8

300 g/10½ oz streaky (lean) bacon
1 large onion, chopped
1 loaf of cheap white bread, crusts removed and sliced into triangles
2 x jars of tomato or taco sauce (about 800 g/1 lb 12 oz)
150 g/5 oz/1⅓ cups Cheddar cheese, grated
salt and black pepper
4 eggs
about 250 ml/9 fl oz/generous 1 cup milk

Preheat the oven to 160°C/325°F/Gas Mark 3.

Start by cutting up the bacon into small pieces and frying (without oil) until crispy. Remove the bacon from the pan and cook the onion in the bacon fat until soft.

Meanwhile, place a layer of bread across the bottom of a large lasagne dish, so the dish is covered. Spread one-third of the sauce across the bread, then sprinkle with the cheese, onion and bacon. Season each layer as you go. Repeat for another two layers.

Whisk the eggs and milk together and pour across the dish, then allow to soak in. You can do this night before if you are organized. If the top looks dry add more milk.

Bake for 30–40 minutes, or until it is puffy and golden brown.

WHISKY PORRIDGE

We originally prepared this recipe as part of the 12-course (4,000 calorie) *Victorian Breakfast* at Warwick Castle. It was a vast meal based on a menu once served to Queen Victoria on a train. This whisky porridge kicked things off to a roaring start. Victorians thought of their stomachs as amiable gentlemen; well-liked uncles who would behave magnificently if treated with respect. You should too.

SERVES 8

750 ml/1¼ pints/3 cups water
750 ml/1¼ pints/3 cups full cream (whole) milk (with more milk to serve - to taste)
750 g/1lb 10 oz/generous 8¾ cups medium ground oats
pinch of salt
whisky (use whatever brand you like)
demerara (raw brown) sugar

Bring the water and milk to the boil and pour in the oats. Stir vigorously with a wooden spoon and, once back on the boil, cover the pan, reduce the heat and simmer very gently for 10 minutes. Add the salt at this point and simmer for a further 5 minutes or so. It should be a thick but pourable consistency.

We serve it from a silver soup tureen with a silver sugar sifter, but use whatever you have. Ceremoniously bring the porridge to the table and anoint with a shower of whisky. Serve with milk and demerara (raw brown) sugar.

CHILLED GRAPEFRUIT WITH CRÈME DE MENTHE

Followers of celebrity dieticians always start breakfast with fruit. However, when you are trying to get over last night, something stronger is more suitable. The Victorians had this cunning dish to get you shamelessly on your way. It's also about the only sensible use for crème de menthe.

PER PERSON
1 red grapefuit
2 mint sprigs
healthy splash of crème de menthe

Cut the grapefruit in half around its equator. Now, armed with a novel grapefruit knife, stealthily remove the flesh, keeping the shell intact. Carefully part the segments from any membrane. Take one of the half-shells and arrange your segments in them marking the centre with the mint. Just before serving sprinkle generously with the crème de menthe.

GIRVAN BRICK

Breakfast rolls don't get more full on than this. At its heart is the mighty "slice o' lorne": ubiquitous in Scotland, but rare elsewhere. Sliced lorne sausage is spicy and dense. The addition of egg and cheese turbocharge it. This is an Egg McMuffin for those in denial.

For this to pop you need to get decent lorne and black pudding slices. Ramsay of Carluke excels in both and you can order online (see Suppliers). The demi brioche roll is a posh burger bun. It is futile to attempt making them yourself. If you can't find such a thing get the shiniest looking burger bun you can find (certainly *not* a floury bap).

PER BRICK

1 slice black pudding (blood sausage)

4-cm/1½-in demi brioche roll with sesame seeds

butter, for greasing

1 egg

salt and black pepper

1 slice lorne sausage

groundnut (peanut) oil, for frying

1 tsp cucumber ketchup (see p.207)

1 tsp black champagne sauce (see p.207)

1 tsp Stichelton or blue cheese

Preheat the oven to 160°C/325°F/Gas Mark 3.

Start by slicing the black pudding (blood sausage), arranging on a metal tray and baking in the oven for about 20 minutes or so until cooked through.

Meanwhile, slice your rolls and butter some ramekins (one for every roll). Crack an egg into each ramekin and season with salt and pepper. Bake each egg in the oven for about 8 minutes, or until the white is set. Remove the eggs from the oven and cover the ramekins loosely with foil.

Fry the slice of lorne in a little oil until crispy on the outside and cooked through, about 8 minutes.

To assemble the brick

Remove the egg from the ramekins by running a knife all around the edge and tipping out. Spread some cucumber ketchup on the bottom of the roll and some black champagne sauce on the top. Place a slice of lorne, then the black pudding and then the egg onto the bottom half. Finally, spread some cheese onto the inside of the top bun.

Wrap each bun in a linen napkin and serve with a cup of strong milky tea.

DOUGHNUT BACON BUTTY

For a shocking but rational breakfast snack the doughnut bacon butty is an easy winner. First developed for our Monnow Valley Drive Thru, this American-inspired breakfast sounds abysmal but tastes like someone has taken a hammer of pleasure to your tongue.

PER BUTTY

3 slices smoked dry cured back (Canadian) bacon

1 "chocolate sprinkles" Krispy Kreme doughnut

1 tsp tomato ketchup or brown sauce

2 slices of tomato

Preheat the grill (broiler) to high.

Fry the bacon and keep warm. Carefully slice the doughnut using a serrated knife, be careful to keep the glaze as intact as possible. Grill (broil) the inside of the doughnut so that it is lightly toasted. When toasted, spread the ketchup on the bottom of the doughnut and top with the bacon and the tomato. Close the lid.

Serve on a plate lined with a paper napkin. More than one per person would be disgusting.

SEATTLE DUTCH BABY

After a savoury bread 'n' butter pudding (see p.186) we need a sweet Yorkshire pudding recipe. This magnificent pimped-out pancake is always impressive.

SERVES 8
120 g/4 oz/1 stick/½ cup unsalted butter
6 eggs
350 ml/12 fl oz/1½ cups milk
180 g/6½ oz/generous 1¼ cups plain (all purpose) flour
icing (confectioners') sugar, for dusting

FOR THE TOPPING
Mixed fruit, chopped, e.g. strawberries, blueberries, bananas...

Preheat the oven to 220°C/425°F/Gas Mark 7.

First choose your dish to bake the Dutch Baby in. We like to use a large sauté pan, about 5½ cm/14 in in diameter, but a roasting tray with high sides or a ceramic oven dish will also work.

Heat the dish along with the oven and, when up to temperature, throw in the butter to melt. While it is melting, use a blender to mix the eggs and milk together. Gradually add the flour until you get a batter.

Carefully pour the batter into the dish. Close the door and cook for about 25 minutes.

When it is cooked remove from the oven and dust with icing (confectioners') sugar. Pile on the chopped fruit and serve.

ACCOMPANIMENTS

BOILED POTATO BONES

These potatoes are carved to look like little bones. They are inspired by a dish at Arzak in San Sebastián in Spain that was so good Sam almost proposed to his girlfriend. When we do them they look like a freaky vegetarian homage to Fergus Henderson. We like to stuff the potato bones with mushroom ketchup (see p.207) for the full effect.

PER PERSON
2 medium-sized potatoes
salt
2 tsp mushroom ketchup
(see p.207)

Start by peeling the potatoes. Then, cut off the bottoms so that they stand upright. Using a paring knife, carve the potato into a cylinder about 3 cm/1¼ in wide. Keep the potatoes in a bowl of water as you go. Take each cylinder and carve it into a bone shape by thinning the middle. You can be as creative as you like. Finish by using a melon baller to scoop out a hollow in the top of each bone. This will later be filled with the mushroom ketchup.

Simmer the prepared potatoes in salted water. Keep the water simmering very gently, it should just be steaming a little. The potatoes will take longer to cook this way but it will keep their shape intact. When the potatoes are cooked (check with a knife) remove them with a slotted spoon and stand upright on a tray. Allow to dry for a few minutes, then fill the hollows with the mushroom ketchup. If necessary you can keep the potatoes warm in a low oven; standing them upright in an ovenproof saucepan sealed with a piece of clingfilm (plastic wrap) is the best method.

POMMES ANNA

If you want to flatter an honoured guest follow the lead of chefs through history and cunningly change the name of the dish to theirs. They will feel a bit special and you can claim the laurels for creating it in their honour. So if we were cooking this for our all-time horror hero and cookbook author Vincent Price, we'd call it *Pommes Vincent*. Given that he's responsible for films like the masterful *House of Wax*, the "rap" on Michael Jackson's *Thriller* and his transition to cookery writer and connoisseur in booming post-war America, he's a man who well deserves the honour. Vincent Price's cookbook *A Treasury of Great Recipes* sees him hit the greatest restaurants in the world and bag their recipes. It also shows you how to fold napkins like lotus flowers, palms, lilies and cacti and recommends entertaining guests by your pool.

Classically this dish is made solely with potatoes and butter, but the dates and chicken stock make for a more rounded flavour. It's a good potato dish to make in advance.

SERVES 8

2 kg/4 lb 8 oz potatoes
salt
pepper
2 shallots, finely diced
10 medjool dates, stoned and finely diced
150 ml/5 fl oz/^{2}/$_3$ cup chicken stock
salt
250 g/9 oz/1 ^{1}/$_8$ cups butter

Peel the potatoes and slice thinly into rounds. A mandoline, set at 1.5 mm/^{5}/$_8$ in is ideal for this. Rinse the slices and pat dry with kitchen paper (paper towels). Cook the dates and the shallots in the chicken stock in a small pan for about 10 minutes. The aim is to evaporate out the stock. Season with a little salt.

Clarify the butter by melting it in a small pan and then skimming off the solids at the top. Pour about 50 g/1^3/$_4$ oz/3^1/$_2$ tbsp of the clarified butter into the base of an ovenproof frying pan that will take all the potatoes. Arrange a layer of potatoes around the base in a neat overlapping circle and spread a thin layer of the date mix on top, leaving a border from the edge. Season the layer lightly and continue with another layer of potatoes and dates. Keep adding layers until all the potatoes are used up, finishing with a plain layer of potatoes. Pour over the remainder of the clarified butter, then put the pan over a gentle heat and cook for a few minutes until the butter starts to bubble and there are some signs of browning. Transfer the pan to an oven and bake at 170°C/325°F/Gas Mark 3 for about 45 minutes.

When done, remove from the oven and allow to cool for a few minutes. Run a knife around the edge of the pan and un-mould onto a plate. The potatoes can be prepared to this stage in advance and then reheated in a hot oven for 15 minutes when needed.

CELERIAC, LEEK AND POTATO GRATIN

This gratin is a trusty side that works well as a main course if you are ambushed by unexpected vegetarians at the table. The problem is that it's so tasty your regular meat-eaters might pretend to be vegetarian to get in on the action. We ended up in a pickle one night doing a dinner for ten with a fixed menu. It didn't look like it would be tricky until four of them turned out to be vegetarians who hadn't told us in advance. To make matters worse we were in the middle of nowhere, there were scant ingredients to hand and there were five courses to battle through. When it transpired that another three diners were teetotal we thought we were finished. This dish helped save the day and they enjoyed it so much one diner tried to steal the cutlery as "a memento of the best meal of his life". We got it back (from his top pocket) after an initially awkward conversation and he booked us to cater his next birthday.

SERVES 8

500 g/1 lb 2 oz leeks, trimmed
50 g/1³/₄ oz/3¹/₂ tbsp butter
2 tsp chopped capers
salt and black pepper
1.5 kg/3 lb 5 oz potatoes
1 kg/2 lb 4 oz celeriac (celery root), peeled
600 ml/1 pint/2¹/₂ cups double (heavy) cream
50 g/1³/₄ oz/scant ¹/₄ cup grated Parmesan (optional)

Preheat the oven to 140°C/275°F/Gas Mark 1.

Start by finely slicing the leeks and cooking gently with the butter in a pan until soft. At this point stir in the chopped capers and season with a little salt and pepper. Meanwhile, finely slice the celeriac (celery root) and potatoes into rounds.

Fill the bottom of an oven-to-table dish with half of the cooked leek mixture. Cover with a layer of potatoes and then a layer of celeriac. Season and pour over half of the cream. Repeat the layering process, then sprinkle the Parmesan on the top, if wished.

Cook in the oven for about an hour, then turn the heat up as necessary towards the end of the cooking time to crispen the top.

MEDIEVAL GREENS

This dish is about as historic as Medieval Times, but it does the trick and is an excellent accompaniment for roast meat. If you can get it served by hot wenches alongside gallons of mead it'll contribute to a glorious dinner adventure. Boil the greens in advance to get ahead and then reheat with the butter, spices and sultanas (golden raisins).

SERVES 8

salt
1 kg/2 lb 4 oz greens
50 g/1³/₄ oz/3¹/₂ tbsp butter
¹/₂ freshly grated nutmeg
1 tsp ground cinnamon
20 g/³/₄ oz/generous ¹/₈ cup sultanas (golden raisins)

Have a bowl filled with iced water ready. Get out the largest pan that you have, fill with water and bring to the boil. Add salt so that the water tastes like the sea. Boil the greens in batches for about 5 minutes, or until cooked through. If the water goes off the boil when you add the veg you are adding too many at once. Remove the greens with a strainer and plunge into the iced water. Once cool, drain and refrigerate.

When you are ready to serve, put a large pan on the heat and add the butter, nutmeg, cinnamon and sultanas. When the butter is hot, add the greens and stir thoroughly for about 5 minutes to reheat.

BOILED ROMANESCO CAULIFLOWER

This brassica is totally trippy - we call it an LSD cauliflower, which makes ordering from the greengrocer interesting. Its fractal pattern is beautiful and, served whole, it makes an impressive and easy dish.

SERVES 8

1 romanesco cauliflower

FOR THE DRESSING

50 ml/1^3/$_4$ fl oz/scant ^{1}/$_4$ cup olive oil
1 tsp finely chopped capers
1 tsp finely chopped red onion
1 tbsp white wine vinegar
salt, to taste

Bring a pan of water, large enough to hold the whole cauliflower, to the boil. Strip the cauliflower of any leaves and cut the stalk down as low as possible, taking care to keep the structure intact. Boil for about 7 minutes, or until tender.

Meanwhile, mix all the dressing ingredients together and, when ready, drain the cauliflower and pour the dressing over while still hot.

Serve the cauliflower whole, inviting your guests to portion it themselves.

BLUE CHEESE, LEEKS AND COGNAC-FLAMED MUSHROOMS

Tasty, but not healthy, this is recipe makes a good filling for a vol-au-vent to dish out to those vegetarians.

SERVES 6

500 g/1 lb 2 oz leeks, trimmed and sliced into 1-cm/½-in rings
salt and black pepper
25 g/1 oz/2 tbsp butter
200 g/7 oz button (white) mushrooms, cut into quarters
1 bunch of thyme
50 ml/1¾ fl oz/scant ¼ cup Cognac

FOR THE SAUCE

50 g/1¾ oz/3½ tbsp butter
25 g/1 oz/2 tbsp plain (all-purpose) flour
800 ml/1½ pints/scant 3½ cups full fat (whole) milk, warmed
200 g/7 oz Stilton or other blue cheese, crumbled

Have a large bowl filled with iced water ready. Blanch the leeks for 5 minutes in a large pan of heavily salted boiling water. Remove with a slotted spoon and cool in the iced water. Once cool, drain and set aside.

Add the 25 g/1 oz/2 tbsp butter to a saucepan and, once melted, add the mushrooms, seasoning them liberally with salt and pepper. Throw the thyme on top and cook until the mushrooms have shrunk and show a good bit of brown. Throw in the Cognac and set alight. After about 10 seconds the flames should have subsided. Tip out the mushrooms onto a tray to cool.

In a heavy-based saucepan, add the 50 g/1¾ oz/3½ tbsp butter and melt over a low heat. Add the flour and stir to form a roux. Keep cooking over a very gentle heat for a few minutes. Gradually incorporate the warm milk and keep whisking and stirring to form a smooth white sauce. Cook for a further 20 minutes until the sauce thickens and everything is perfectly smooth. Add the cheese, then stir until it has melted. Season, then tip into a bowl to cool. This can all be done in advance.

To reheat, combine the cheese sauce with the leeks and mushrooms (remove the thyme) and cook gently, stirring constantly until back up to temperature. Serve as a side dish or, for a complete dish, use as the filling for a vol-au-vent (see pp.211-3).

CARAMELIZED FENNEL AND ONIONS

As food became more readily available at the beginning of the twentieth century, concern started to emerge that it could have negative effects on the body. Prior to this, being dangerously overweight was generally considered to be the result of bad luck for which there was, sadly, no cure. Further back still, obesity had been an enviable characteristic, signalling the wealth of its bearer. Men of a certain contour and profile were the heroes of the day.

As the connection was made between eating and weight gain, ingenious and imaginative, if not always practical, ways of avoiding this side-effect began to appear, giving rise to what is now the diet industry. Indeed, fad diets are not a new concept at all. William Banting wrote the first ever diet book based on a low carbohydrate plan in the mid-1800s. In the early twentieth century, weight-loss ideas flourished, ranging from the most obvious – fasting (also put forward as an antidote for emaciation by American writer Upton Sinclair) – to the ridiculous. Horace Fletcher, the "Great Masticator's" popular doctrine was that chewing was the answer. He suggested that food should be chewed until it turned to liquid and that even liquids needed chewing a few times. Other "healthy" regimes included cigarette and drinking diets. One of our favourites is the Champagne diet recommended by Joan Oliphant-Fraser. This is the perfect dish for a Champagne diet alongside magnums all day.

SERVES EITHER 8 OR 4
4 fennel bulbs
4 medium-sized onions
salt
50 g/1³/₄ oz/3¹/₂ tbsp butter
25 g/1 oz/2 tbsp brown sugar
100 ml/3¹/₂ fl oz/generous ¹/₄ cup white wine vinegar

Preheat the oven to 150°C/300°F/Gas Mark 2.

Cut the fennel into quarters, freshening up the cut stalk end but keeping everything attached together. Quarter the onions between the poles and peel. Don't remove the core or the onions will fall apart and you want to keep them together.

Blanch the fennel in a pan of boiling salted water for about 8 minutes, then drain in a colander. Meanwhile, in a heavy (and ideally ovenproof) saucepan, melt the butter and add the sugar. Lay in the onions and cook over a moderate heat so that they start to caramelize. Once the onions are showing some good colour, add in the blanched fennel and continue cooking in the same manner. Turn everything gently so that each piece of veg stays as one.

Next, add the vinegar and reduce by about half. Place the pan in the oven for about 15 minutes to finish cooking. If you make this in advance, reheat by placing back in the oven for 20 minutes.

CUCUMBER KETCHUP

1 shallot, finely diced
1 cucumber, peeled and finely diced
1 tsp mustard seeds,
tied in a muslin bag
100 ml/3$\frac{1}{2}$ fl oz/generous $\frac{1}{3}$ cup
white wine vinegar
100 g/3$\frac{1}{2}$ oz/$\frac{1}{2}$ cup granulated
sugar

This is a good alternative for gherkins in burgers.

Add all the ingredients to a small saucepan. Bring to the boil and boil rapidly for about 10 minutes. It should end up fairly sticky and thick. Remove the mustard seeds and pass the cucumber mixture through a food mill. This will keep for a few days in the fridge.

MUSHROOM KETCHUP

500 g/1 lb 2 oz button (white) mushrooms, finely diced
1 shallot, finely diced
1$\frac{1}{2}$ tbsp sea salt
125 ml/4 fl oz/$\frac{1}{2}$ cup white wine vinegar
1 tsp ground ginger
$\frac{1}{2}$ tsp ground nutmeg
500 ml/1 pint/2 cups chicken stock
black pepper

Ideal for serving with boiled potatoes (see p.198).

Start by salting the mushrooms so that the juices come out. Combine the mushrooms, shallots and sea salt in a bowl and cover with clingfilm (plastic wrap). Leave for a couple of days.

Throw the mushrooms and their liquid into a saucepan and add the vinegar and spices. Boil rapidly until there's about a tablespoon of liquid left. Add the chicken stock, bring to the boil and simmer until most of the liquid has boiled off. Use a food processor to purée the mushrooms. Season with black pepper. The ketchup will keep for a couple of weeks in the fridge.

BLACK CHAMPAGNE SAUCE

100 ml/3$\frac{1}{2}$ fl oz/generous $\frac{1}{3}$ cup vermouth (eg. Noilly Prat)
1 small shallot, finely diced
100 ml/3$\frac{1}{2}$ fl oz/generous $\frac{1}{3}$ cup HP sauce (brown sauce)
100 ml/3$\frac{1}{2}$ fl oz/generous $\frac{1}{3}$ cup Champagne

We like to think this is a bastardisation of an Agnes B. Marshall recipe, but we may well have made the whole thing up. The best bit is that it's totally mysterious if you stay quiet about the ingredients.

Add the vermouth and the shallots to a small saucepan and cook gently until the shallots are soft and translucent and the vermouth has reduced by half. Add the HP sauce and the Champagne and continue cooking until reduced by a third. Strain, cool and refrigerate until required. It will keep for a few days.

MAYONNAISE

Decent homemade mayonnaise is the basis for so many good things. It is worth mastering the technique.

MAKES ABOUT
250 G/9 OZ/GENEROUS 1 CUP
1 egg yolk
1 tsp white wine vinegar
1 tsp mustard powder
pinch of salt
250 ml/9 fl oz/generous 1 cup groundnut (peanut) oil/olive oil (not extra virgin olive oil)

For the mayonnaise

In the small bowl of a food processor fitted with the standard blade, add the egg yolk, vinegar, mustard and salt. Blitz for a few seconds to incorporate. With the motor running, add the oil, drop by drop. When you've added 50 ml/1¾ fl oz/ scant ¼ cup of the oil the sauce should be looking homogenous and the oil fully incorporated. At this point you can add the oil in a very slow stream but always erring on the side of caution. You will end up with a thick yellow mayonnaise. If you have electric beaters you can make the mayonnaise with them instead. It's less washing up.

- THINGS TO DO WITH THE MAYONNAISE -

FOR CELERIAC REMOULADE
1 lemon
400 g/14 oz celeriac (celery root)
125 g/4 oz/½ cup mayonnaise (see above)
2 tsp chopped capers
1 tsp chopped flat-leaf parsley
1 tsp finely chopped tarragon
salt

Remoulade

Celeriac is the classic "remoulade" but it is easy enough to think of other ingredients that take the shredding and mayonnaise treatment well.

For celeriac remoulade

Start by squeezing the lemon into a bowl. Peel the celeriac (celery root) and cut into manageable chunks. Using a mandoline, cut the celeriac into fine julienne pieces and immediately add the cut celeriac to the lemon juice to stop it discolouring. Mix the mayonnaise, capers and herbs together and season with a pinch of salt. Mix the mayonnaise through with the celeriac. Keep refrigerated until ready to serve.

FOR CRABSLAW

100 g/3½ oz carrots
100 g/3½ oz red onions
100 g/3½ oz fennel
100 g/3½ oz/generous ⅓ cup mayonnaise (see above)
100 g/3½ oz picked white crabmeat
1 tsp finely chopped parsley
1 tsp finely chopped chervil
juice of ½ lemon

Crabslaw

This recipe was first suggested in our cocktail book, but it's a good thing and may give you gout. So here it is again.

Peel the carrots and cut into thin slices using a mandoline. Roughly cut lengthways to create thinner pieces. Run the fennel and onions through the mandoline and cut into thin slices. Mix all remaining ingredients together and use to bind the sliced vegetables.

FOR SALAD DRESSING

100 g/3½ oz/generous ⅓ cup mayonnaise (see above)
1 tsp finely chopped chervil
1 tsp finely chopped tarragon
1 tsp finely chopped oregano
juice of 1 lemon
50 ml/1¾ fl oz/scant ¼ cup water

Salad dressing

Let down the mayonnaise with the lemon juice and water, then stir in the herbs. Adjust seasoning to taste.

FOR TARTAR SAUCE

150 g/5 oz/⅔ cup mayonnaise (see above)
1 hard-boiled egg, finely chopped
3 tsp finely chopped capers
3 tsp finely chopped cornichons
2 tsp finely chopped parsley

Tartar sauce

Simply stir all the ingredients together.

TECHNIQUE FOR
PERFECT SCRAMBLED EGGS

8 eggs

75 g/2³/₄ oz/6 tbsp unsalted butter

In a small saucepan, crack in eight eggs and a really good slab of unsalted butter, about 75 g/2³/₄ oz/6 tbsp. Cut the butter into a few slices to help it melt. Quality of eggs and butter is important so use the best you can find. Put the pan on a very gentle heat. If you're using gas put it on the slowest smallest ring. With a wooden spatula, poke the yolks so that they break and give everything a thorough mix. If you see white firming up you've got it on way too high a heat. Continue beating the eggs together while cooking. What you are aiming for is to thicken the eggs so that it gets to a stage where it's forming soft curds. You shouldn't be scraping solid bits off the bottom of the pan and incorporating them - if this happens the heat is too strong. When you reach this stage (kind of like a really runny omelette) take the pan off the heat and continue to stir. The egg will carry on cooking but it will relax at the same time. What will happen is that the bits that have firmed up will go more liquid and the liquid bits will firm up a little.

After about 30 seconds the pan can go back on the heat. Keep stirring until the mixture thickens again - this time it should be more uniform. Now is the time to add a tiny pinch of salt. At this point you can cook the eggs to the way you like them. Ideally, they should be very soft curds and at a point where they can just about maintain some shape. Take the pan off the heat before the eggs are done and continue to stir. Serve at once.

Making decent scrambled eggs this way is difficult with fewer than three eggs and more than about twelve. This is because with too few the heat rips through the eggs too quickly and with too many the eggs build up too much heat retention and it is difficult to control the outcome - it tends to go from too liquid to too solid in a matter of seconds.

TECHNIQUE FOR PUFF PASTRY

The secret of making puff pastry is to allow lots of time and to keep everything chilled. If you are not in it for the long haul, skip to another recipe. On a similar thread this is not a summertime recipe. So if it's a hot day, it's best to avoid the inevitable grief. Our kitchen is normally so chilly that it is perfect for making pastry. For added security Harry likes to put a marble rolling slab in the refrigerator to cool down between turns. Incidentally when he first started making puff pastry he liked to use a chilled can of Red Stripe lager as the rolling pin – functional, cheap and refreshing. For this recipe you should use a rolling pin that is about 30 cm/12 in long.

Puff pastry is composed of hundreds of thin leaves of pastry dough interleaved with butter. In total you will be attempting to make 1,459 layers of pastry and butter, so as you may imagine there is scope for error. All these layers should make for a hearty rise as the pastry cooks. We always make vol-au-vents in advance. Once cooled they keep for a few days in a large tin and they also freeze well.

MAKES ONE 20-CM/8-IN VOL-AU-VENT AND 40 CHEESE STRAWS

500 g/1 lb 2 oz/3½ cups plain (all purpose) flour, plus extra for dusting

1 tsp salt

500 g/1 lb 2 oz/scant 2½ cups chilled unsalted butter, grated

about 150 ml/5 fl oz/⅔ cup iced water

1 tsp lemon juice

1 egg beaten with 1 tsp water

The dough

Sift 450 g/1 lb/scant 3½ cups of the flour into the bowl of a food mixer. Add the salt and mix on a low speed using the normal mixer blade (eg the Kenwood K blade). Gradually add 50 g/1¾ oz/3½ tbsp of the grated butter. Mix thoroughly for about 5 minutes, or until you can feel that the butter has been cut down into small pieces.

Meanwhile, mix the water and lemon juice together. Throw in a bunch of ice cubes to chill the water. Slowly add the water until a dough starts to form. You may need to add slightly more or less water. When the dough starts to come together add a touch more water and then stop. Remove from the bowl and push together with your hand to form a ball. Fold over a couple of times to make sure that it is one homogenous whole. Wrap in cling film (plastic wrap) and refrigerate. Let the dough rest for at least half an hour.

The butter

While the dough is resting make up the butter ready to be rolled into all those layers. The aim is to combine 450 g/1 lb/2 cups of butter with 50 g/1¾ oz/generous ⅓ cup of flour. Clean out the bowl of the mixer. Place 50 g/1¾ oz/generous ⅓ cup of flour in the bottom of the bowl and add the grated butter on top. You will need to push the butter down to make room for it all. Fit the

dough hook to the machine and mix until everything is combined. You may need to occasionally pull the butter off the hook if it masses up. Don't overmix, but make sure that it is all well combined.

Mould the butter mix into a square about 8 x 8 cm/3 x 3 in. Wrap in cling film and place in the refrigerator to firm up a little.

Combining the dough and butter
Flour the work surface and rolling pin and roll out the dough into a 30-cm/12-in diameter circle. Place the butter square in the middle and fold over the dough so that it covers the butter. Push together with your hands. It should overlap a decent amount.

Check that everything is still floured and then roll out the pastry parcel so that it is about 40 cm/16 in long and 20 cm/8 in wide. Take the top third of the dough and fold it over and then bring up the bottom third and place on top. A bit like folding a letter to fit an envelope. Turn the whole lot 90 degrees to the left, check the flour situation and roll out again to the 40 x 20 cm/16 x 8 in size, and do the same folding action. Now you have given the dough two folds. In total there will be six layers.

Refrigerate for at least half an hour and then repeat the operation above. If the dough appears very soft put it back in the refrigerator.

Repeat the double rolling and folding one last time to make all six manoeuvers. The dough will be getting soft and fragile by this point, so if you can let it rest for longer before the final two rolls then so much the better.

After all six turns have been completed, rest the dough for a further hour before rolling out.

Forming the vol-au-vent
Roll out the pastry to create a 40 x 28-cm/16 x 11-in rectangle. The pastry should be a chunky 1 cm/½ in thick. Find a circular template (cake tin/plate/bowl) 20 cm/8 in in diameter and cut two circles from the pastry. The circles should be cut from well within the borders of the sheet, otherwise the rise will be uneven. Use a sharp knife to cut the pastry as you don't want to compress the layers of pastry together. Pull off the trimmed outside rectangle, place flat on a tray and put back into the refrigerator. Later this could become cheese straws (see p.58) or the base of a tarte tatin (p.135). Take one of the circles and cut out a circle, 14 cm/5½ in diameter from the centre. You should now have two circles of pastry and a ring of pastry.

Carefully move the larger circle to the centre of a cool baking sheet. Use a pastry brush to brush a ring of water around the edge, the same size as the pastry ring. To move the ring on top of the circle you need to fold it loosely in half and then into quarters. This will stop it stretching. Align it with the base, unfold it and press lightly into position.

Cover loosely with cling film and refrigerate for half an hour before decorating and baking.

Preheat the oven to 210°C/410°F/Gas Mark 6.

Decoration
Just before cooking decorate the vol-au-vent. Using a knife, scallop the edges and make some radial marks on top. Score the interior lightly, making a cut about 5 mm/¼ in deep all around the interior into the bottom layer of the pastry. Score a criss-cross pattern lightly onto the base. Later this will become the lid. Prick the pastry in about 8 places with a knife to help it to rise. Brush the top and inside floor with the egg wash. Do not get egg on any side walls or you will stick the pastry together and it won't get off the ground.

Baking
Bake in the centre of the oven for a total of 50 minutes. After 20 minutes turn the heat down to 180°C/350°F/Gas Mark 4 and continue cooking the pastry through without burning. It is likely that the very bottom of the vol-au-vent may burn slightly but this is unavoidable.

Remove from the oven and, using a palette knife, attempt to carefully remove the lid. This is not always successful but is worth trying. If it goes wrong, you may as well eat it now, if it comes out in one piece, hurrah - save it for later. You will notice that the inside of the vol-au-vent contains some uncooked pastry. Use a teaspoon to scrape this out. Return the vol-au-vent to the oven for another 5 minutes to finish cooking the inside.

See p.92 for a recipe to fill the finished vol-au-vent.

HOW TO LOLLIPOP
A CHICKEN

Chicken lollipops are as silly as they sound. If you can get the hang of the technique it will seriously up your kitchen gamesmanship. It's easy enough to do.

First, we like to open the chicken up a bit. Chickens nearly always come trussed so start by cutting off the string with a pair of kitchen scissors. Then sit the chicken upright and flex it joints. Bring its wings out and in, as if you are making it do some freaky meat aerobics. Do the same with the wings. Now when you put the chicken back on the chopping (cutting) board it will look more like an animal with its limbs all relaxed. This ridiculous set of moves makes it easier to see what you are doing when you start to cut it up.

Start by removing the wings. Chop through the joint so that you take a little slice of the breast meat with it. This makes it easier to make a clean cut and gives a better portion to eat. You will have two wing sections that have three joints. From the wing tip find the second joint and then move your knife about 5 mm/ ¼ in in the direction of the wing tip so that it is directly over the bone rather than the joint. Cut through at this point. You'll be going through bone so you need to be decisive. The next bit is a little tricky to explain but is a top move.

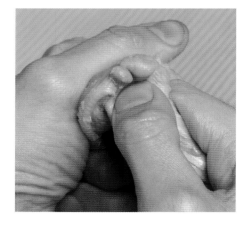

Take the wing section attached to the tip. Bend over the wing tip to the side so that the bone pops out of place. With your thumb on the now dislocated wing tip push the tip down so that the two bones of the next section break through the skin. Push the meat all the way down the two bones and over the end so that the meat is inverted. Then cut off the wing tip and trim away the excess piece of fat hanging on. You will be left with a piece of meat with two bones sticking out of it. Pull the smaller bone out. Your first lollipop is ready.

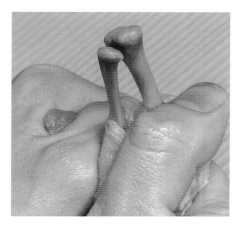

You now need to make another lollipop from the remaining wing section. This one is a bit more basic. The wing piece will have two small bone stubs sticking out of it where you cut it through. Run a knife around the joint and wiggle it through to remove these.

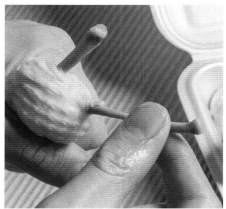

Place the chicken on a large chopping board breast up. Take off the legs by running a knife through the skin down towards the bottom of the breasts. At this point I like to tug the leg so that the socket comes out and then another push of the blade and the leg is off. Take each leg and cut through the joint to remove the drumstick from the thigh. Again the cheat's way is to snap the joint to show you where to cut. I then like to slice off about half the flesh from the thigh to create two pieces of meat - one with bone, the other without. With the drumstick you need to first remove the final "shin" bit. Again snap the joint and carefully remove the last limb.

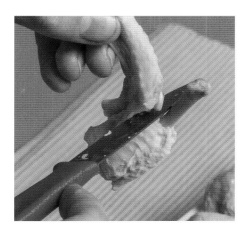

Finally, to make the meat cook in a proper Fred Flintstone style, you need to cut through the sinews that hold the meat onto the full extend of the drumstick. At the end where the bone sticks out, run a knife around the skin and push down the flesh and skin so that the bone is revealed. Carefully cut out any sinews that remain. If you feel like it you should really remove the sinews by pulling them out with a pair of pliers.

Recipes using this technique can be found on pages 61 and 94.

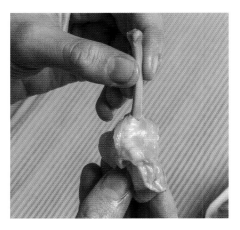

INDEX

Page numbers in **bold** denote
an illustration

absinthe
eagle tail **174**, 175
lime and absinthe jelly 116
alchemical mountain brew 166–8, **167**
almonds, spiced roast **56**, 57
anchovies
surrealist stuffed eggs 60
apples
tarte tatin **134**, 135
architectural food 16
Armagnac
floc de Gascogne 165
Artisanal Chewing Gum Factory
(Whiteleys, London) 145, 147
asparagus
surrealist stuffed eggs 60
atmospheres, enriched 142–3

B&P cocktail 165
bacon
bread 'n' breakfast pudding 186
clam chowder 86, **87**
creamed smoked haddock with bacon
and peas in a vol-au-vent 92, **93**
doughnut bacon butty 192, **193**
banana flambé **120**, 121
basil seeds
mock turtle soup with perfumed
quail's eggs **78**, 79
beef
braised beef shin 106, **107**
cow pie **108**, 109
medieval roast 110, **111**
steak tartare **72**, 73
Billings, C.K.G. 14
biscuits, boudoir **136**, 137
Black Banquet (1783) 26
black champagne sauce 207
black pudding
girvan brick **190**, 191

blancmange, coconut 122
blue cheese, leeks and Cognac flamed
mushrooms 205
boiled potato bones 198
boiled romanesco cauliflower 202
Bonvalet, Monsieur 13
boudoir biscuits **136**, 137
braised beef shin 106, **107**
brandy
eagle tail **174**, 175
bread 'n' breakfast pudding 186
brioche roll
girvan brick **190**, 191
bush of crayfish in viking herbs 82–5, **83**
butter
grilled soles with maître d'hôtel **90**, 91
potted crab **74**, 75
potted mushrooms 76, **77**

Campari
and orange jelly marble 125
veneziano cocktail 162, **163**
canapés
cheese straws 58, **59**
chicken lollipops 61
frog's legs 67, **67**
pastel sandwiches 62, **63**
quail's eggs with chilli & 24 carat gold
54, **55**
smoked eel, celeriac remoulade and
oatcake **68**, 69
snails en attelet 65–6
spiced roast almonds **56**, 57
surrealist stuffed eggs 60
candied roses 128, **129**
caped turkey **98**, 99
capers
boiled romanesco cauliflower 202
celeriac, leek and potato gratin 200
celeriac remoulade 208
tartar sauce 209
caramelized fennel and onions 206
Carême, Antonin 16, **17**

carrots
crabslaw 209
cauliflower, boiled romanesco 202
celeriac
celeriac, leek and potato gratin 200
remoulade 208
smoked eel, celeriac remoulade and
oatcake **68**, 69
champagne
black champagne sauce 207
fruit salad of death 172, **173**
champagne towers 180–1, **181**
cheese
blue cheese, leeks and Cognac flamed
mushrooms 205
bread 'n' breakfast pudding 186
celeriac, leek and potato gratin 200
straws 58, **59**
chewing gum 145–7, **146**
chicken
lollipops 61, 214–5
tropical 94, **95**
chieftain pancakes 184, **185**
chilled grapefruit with crème de menthe
188, **189**
chilli
quail's eggs with chilli & 24 carat gold
54, **55**
chorizo
surrealist stuffed eggs 60
chowder, clam/corn 86, **87**
cigarettes 144
clam chowder 86, **87**
cocktails
alchemical mountain brew 166–8, **167**
B&P 165
eagle tail **174**, 175
floc de Gascogne 165
of the future 176–8, **177**
khat 160, **161**
milkshake Alexandra 158, **159**
tentacle martini 179
veneziano 162, **163**

white port and Indian tonic 162

see also punch

coconut blancmange 122

Cognac

    B&P cocktail 165

    blue cheese, leeks and Cognac flamed mushrooms 205

colour, effect of on appetite 35

Company of the Trowel 14

confetti cannon 41

coral jelly **126**, 127

corn chowder 86

Courvoisier

    milkshake Alexandra 158, **159**

cow pie **108**, 109

crab, potted **74**, 75

crabslaw 209

cranberry peach marble jelly 127

crayfish

    bush of crayfish in viking herbs 82–5, **83**

cream

    celeriac, leek and potato gratin 200

    clam chowder 86, **87**

    ice cream mélange 117–8, **119**

    surrealist stuffed eggs 60

creamed smoked haddock with bacon and peas in a vol-au-vent 92, **93**

crème de menthe

    chilled grapefruit with 188, **189**

    cocktail of the future 177, **178**

crispy coated chicken lollipops 61

Crowley, Aleister 175

Cuccagna monuments 16–17, **18–19**

cucumber

    goat's curd and cucumber sandwiches 62

    ketchup 207

custard

    techron trifle 114–6, **115**

dates, pommes Anna 199

de la Reynière, Grimod 26

descending table (1750) 13

desserts

    banana flambé 121

    boudoir biscuits **136**, 137

    candied roses 128, **129**

    coral jelly **126**, 127

    ice cream mélange 117–8, **119**

    lanvin meringues 130, **131**

    neon marbled jelly **123**, 125

    rainbow jelly 122–4, **123**

    tarte tatin **134**, 135

    techron trifle 114–6, **115**

dill

    bush of crayfish in viking herbs 82–5, **83**

doughnut bacon butty 192, **193**

eagle tail **174**, 175

eels

    smoked eel, celeriac remoulade and oatcake **68**, 69

eggs

    bread 'n' breakfast pudding 186

    chieftain pancakes 184, **185**

    girvan brick **190**, 191

    mock turtle soup with perfumed quail's **78**, 79

    quail's eggs with chilli & 24 carat gold 54, **55**

    saffron egg mayonnaise sandwiches 62

    scrambled **80**, 81, 210

    sea urchin oeufs brouillés **80**, 81

    Seattle Dutch baby 194, **195**

    steak tartare **72**, 73

    surrealist stuffed 60

ether, syrup of 175

explosives 36–43

    confetti cannon 41

    tabletop fireworks 40

    wedding 41

feasts, greatest historical 12–19

fennel

    caramelized fennel and onions 206

    crabslaw 209

fireworks, tabletop 40

floc de Gascogne 165

flowers 33–5

    edible 34

    messages of 34

    toxic 34–5

frog's legs 67, **67**

fruit

    Seattle Dutch baby 194, **195**

fruit salad of death 172, **173**

gammon

    glitter ham 102, **103**

garlic

    frog's legs 67, **67**

    snails en attelet 65–6

    tropical chicken 94, **95**

gin

    alchemical mountain brew 166–8, **167**

    cocktail of the future 176–8, **177**

    fruit salad of death 172, **173**

    jelly 125

    tentacle martini 179

ginger

    tropical chicken 94, **95**

ginger ale

    yellow fever punch **170**, 171

girvan brick **190**, 191

glitter ham 102, **103**

goat's curd

    and cucumber sandwiches 62

    surrealist stuffed eggs 60

gold

    quail's eggs with chilli & 24 carat 54, **55**

grapefruit

    chilled grapefruit with crème de menthe 188, **189**

gratin, celeriac, leek and potato 200

green chartreuse
    alchemical mountain brew 166–8, **167**
    tentacle martini 179
green tea
    alchemical mountain brew 166–8, **167**
greens, medieval 201
grenadine ripple ice cream 118
grilled soles with maître d'hôtel butter 90, **91**
gum 145–7, **146**

haddock
    creamed smoked haddock with bacon and peas in a vol-au-vent 92, **93**
ham, glitter 102, **103**
Heliogabalus 12
Hell Banquet (1511) 14
herbs
    bush of crayfish in viking 82–5, **83**
horseback dinner (Sherry's) (1903) 14, **14–15**
horseradish
    smoked salmon and horseradish sandwiches 62
HP sauce
    black champagne sauce 207

ice cream
    grenadine ripple 118
    mélange 117–8, **119**
    mint 118
    pineapple 118
Iguanodon Banquet (1853) 20–21, **21**
Indian tonic, white port and 162

Jackson, Andrew 15
jelly
    Campari and orange jelly marble 125
    coral **126**, 127
    cranberry peach marble 127

gin 125
lime 122
lime and absinthe 116
lime jelly marble 125
mango 122
mint jelly marble 125
neon marbled 125
pomegranate 122
rainbow 122–4, **123**
Jelly Banquet (University College London) 22

Kessler, George 12
ketchup
    cucumber 207
    mushroom 207
khat cocktail 160, **161**
kidney, cow pie **108**, 109
kirsch
    eagle tail **174**, 175

ladyfingers **136**, 137
lanvin meringues 130, **131**
leeches 31
leeks
    blue cheese, leeks and Cognac flamed mushrooms 205
    celeriac, leek and potato gratin 200
lemon sole
    grilled soles with maître d'hôtel butter 90, **91**
lime
    and absinthe jelly 116
    jelly 122
    jelly marble 125
lorne sausages
    girvan brick **190**, 191
Loubet, Émile 15

magic 28–31
maître d'hôtel butter, grilled soles with 90, **91**
mango jelly 122

marmalade
    glitter ham 102, **103**
    quails roasted with marmalade and tobacco 96, **97**
    sticky marmalade chicken lollipops 61
    tropical chicken 94, **95**
martini, tentacle 179
mayonnaise 208
    celeriac remoulade 208
    crabslaw 209
    saffron egg mayonnaise sandwiches 62
    salad dressing 209
    surrealist stuffed eggs 60
    tartar sauce 209
medieval greens 201
medieval roast beef 110, **111**
meringues, lanvin 130, **131**
methyl cellulose 145
milk
    bread 'n' breakfast pudding 186
    clam chowder 86, **87**
    ice cream mélange 117–8, **119**
    whisky porridge 187
milkshake Alexandra 158, **159**
mint
    ice cream 118
    jelly marble 125
Mitterrand, François, last supper (1996) 12–13
mock turtle soup with perfumed quail's eggs **78**, 79
mushroom ketchup 207
    boiled potato bones 198
mushrooms
    blue cheese, leeks and Cognac flamed 205
    ketchup 207
    potted 76, **77**

neon marbled jelly **123**, 125
nuts
    spiced roast almonds **56**, 57

oatcake
    smoked eel, celeriac and remoulade
        and **68**, 69
oats
    whisky porridge 187
octopus
    tentacle martini 179
onions
    caramelized fennel and 206
    crabslaw 209
oranges
    banana flambé 121
    Campari and orange jelly marble 125
ortolan 12-13
ox kidney
    cow pie **108**, 109
oxygen enriched atmospheres 142-3

pancakes
    chieftain 184, 185
    Seattle Dutch baby 194, **195**
Paris feast (1901) 15
Paris zoo, dining at (1870) 13
Parmesan cheese
    celeriac, leek and potato gratin 200
    cheese straws 58, **59**
parsley
    grilled soles with mâitre d'hôtel butter
        90, **91**
pastel sandwiches 62
pastillage 152
pastry
    cheese straws 58, **59**
    cow pie **108**, 109
    creamed smoked haddock with bacon
        and peas in a vol-au-vent 92, **93**
    puff pastry technique 211-3
    tarte tatin **134**, 135
peaches
    cranberry peach marble jelly 127
peas
    creamed smoked haddock with bacon
        and peas in a vol-au-vent 92, **93**

pineapples
    alchemical mountain brew 166-8, **167**
    ice cream 118
    tropical chicken 94, **95**
planning 48-9
pomegranate jelly 122
pommes Anna 199
Pompadour, Madame 13
pork, pulled 104, **105**
porridge, whisky 187
port
    B&P cocktail 165
    white port and Indian tonic 162
potatoes
    boiled potato bones 198
    celeriac, leek and potato gratin 200
    mock turtle soup with perfumed
        quail's eggs **78**, 79
    pommes Anna 199
potted crab **74**, 75
potted mushrooms 76, **77**
puff pastry 92
    cheese straws 58, **59**
    creamed smoked haddock with bacon
        and peas in a vol-au-vent 92, **93**
    tarte tatin **134**, 135
    technique for 211-3
pulled pork 104, **105**
punch
    fruit salad of death 172, **173**
    yellow fever **170**, 171

quail's eggs
    with chilli & 24 carat gold 54, **55**
    mock turtle soup with perfumed **78**,
        79
quails roasted with marmalade and
    tobacco 96, **97**

rainbow jelly 122-4, **123**
red vermouth
    veneziano 162, **163**
remoulade, celeriac 208

roast beef, medieval 110, **111**
Roman orgy 12
roses, candied 128, **129**
ruby port
    B&P cocktail 165
rum
    banana flambé 121
    khat cocktail 160, **161**

saffron egg mayonnaise sandwiches 62
salad dressing 209
salmon
    smoked salmon and horseradish
        sandwiches 62
sandwiches, pastel 62, **63**
    goat's curd and cucumber 62
    saffron egg mayonnaise 62
    smoked salmon and horseradish 62
sauces
    black champagne 207
    tartar 209
    see also ketchup; mayonnaise
sausages
    girvan brick **190**, 191
Savoy Gondola Banquet (1905) 12, **13**
scrambled eggs 81, 210
sea urchin oeufs brouillés **80**, 81
Seattle Dutch baby 194, **195**
service 44-7
sherbet 148, **149**, **150**, **151**
smoked eel, celeriac remoulade and
    oatcake **68**, 69
smoked haddock
    creamed smoked haddock with bacon
        and peas in a vol-au-vent 92, **93**
smoked salmon and horseradish
    sandwiches 62
snails en attelet 65-6
sole
    grilled soles with mâitre d'hôtel butter
        90, **91**
soups
    clam/corn chowder 86, **87**

crayfish 82–5
   mock turtle soup with perfumed
      quail's eggs **78**, 79
southern-fried chicken lollipops 61
spiced roast almonds **56**, 57
spinach
   mock turtle soup with perfumed
      quail's eggs **78**, 79
starters
   bush of crayfish in viking herbs 82–5,
      83
   potted crab **74**, 75
   potted mushrooms 76, **77**
   sea urchin oeufs brouillés **80**, 81
   steak tartare **72**, 73
   see also soups
steak tartare **72**, 73
sugar
   candied roses 128, **129**
   sculpture 152–5
   syrup 122
sultanas
   medieval greens 201
surrealist stuffed eggs 60

table dressing 24–7
tabletop fireworks 40
tartar sauce 209
tarte tatin **134**, 135
techron trifle 114–6, **115**
tentacle martini 179
teriyaki chicken lollipops 61
themes, choosing 20–22
tobacco, quails roasted with marmalade
  and 96, **97**
transglutaminase 145
trifle, techron 114–6, **115**
tropical chicken 94, **95**
turkey, caped **98**, 99

uniform, and waiting staff 44–7

sveneziano 162, **163**
vermouth
   black champagne sauce 207
vodka
   cocktail of the future 178, **179**
vol-au-vent, creamed smoked haddock
   with bacon and peas in a 92, **93**

watercress
   mock turtle soup with perfumed
      quail's eggs **78**, 79
wedding explosions 41
whiskys
   glitter ham 102, **103**
   porridge 187
   yellow fever punch 170, 171
White House cheese fest (1836) 15
white port and Indian tonic 162
white wine
   floc de Gascogne 165
   veneziano 162, **163**

yellow fever punch **170**, 171

SUPPLIERS

Caffeine

You can buy products for transgenics, metabolomics and protomics from Sigma Aldrich, so extremely pure caffeine is tame by comparison.

Sigma Aldrich

http://www.sigmaaldrich.com

+44 (0)800 717181

Food Grade Oxygen

We were first introduced to supplier BOC when hunting for liquid nitrogen to make novelty ice cream. Things started getting really interesting though when we started investigating their catalogue of other chemicals. These are routinely supplied for hospitals, cryogenic bio-storage, the energy industry as well as the food industry. Call them up to order your own canister of food grade oxygen.

BOC

http://www.boconline.co.uk

+44 (0) 800 02 0800

Gold

The European Union designates gold as food additive E175. You could go to a fancy art shop for it but we don't. Ours is from Leyland, the builder's supply merchant. You need to make sure it is over 22 carats to be food safe otherwise you'll be drinking down copper and nickel as well.

L.Cornelissen

www.cornelissen.com

+44 (0) 20 7636 1045

Leyland SDM

www.leylandsdm.co.uk

+44 (0)20 7275 2999

Leeches

Make sure any leeches you buy are medical grade. We buy ours from Biopharm with the reassuring motto 'the biting end of science'. They also sell handy glazed earthenware leech jars modelled on 19th century originals. Each has a perforated lid that allows the leeches to breath but not escape and is topped with a rose-shaped knob. The customer service at Biopharm is extremely good.

Biopharm Leeches

www.biopharm-leeches.com

+44 (0) 1792-885595

Lorne Sausage

Mailorder meat may sound like a horror but rest assured Ramsay of Carluke is an exceptional purveyor of Scottish protein products. The family has been selling meat for 150 years and we turn to him for slice and black, haggis by post and the mighty lorne sausage.

Ramsay of Carluke

www.ramsayofcarluke.co.uk

01555 772 277

Tobacco

Using tobacco in cooking will save your pink lungs while still giving a nicotine fix. Beware that it could also give you cancer. We like to use Black Cavendish tobacco from Smith & Shervingtons in Charing Cross Road. They opened in 1869 so know what they are doing.

Smith & Shervingtons

http://smithsandshervs.com

+44 (0) 20 7836 7422

Staff uniforms

The white carver's jackets sold by Denny's are so dapper Sam has worn them to 10 Downing Street, swanky gallery openings and for important anniversaries as well as to make the largest jelly in the world. Handily, if you get them dirty they can take a savage bleaching. One of the few clothes that swaggers back from death stains. We like to customise ours with fancy collars. Give Denny's hotline a call and see what they can do for you.

Denny's Uniforms

http://www.dennys.co.uk/

+44 (0) 1372377904

Special effects, pyrotechnics, bomb tanks, detonator devices

Stage Electrics is a special effects treasure trove. We look through their catalogues with awe and wonder, puzzling out food applications for their assorted equipment. Could blood packs, snow in a can, UV cannons or ice rinks have any food application?

Stage Electrics

www.stage-electrics.co.uk

+44 (0) 844 870 0077

Weird ingredients: glucose, glycerine, citric acid, tragacanth

If you want trendy or obscure chemicals for cooking, the sort of things 'molecular gastronomers' lust after, give MSK a ring. If they don't have it they will find it.

MSK

www.msk-ingredients.com

+44 (0)1246 412211

BIBLIOGRAPHY

Ballard, J.G. *The Crystal World*, USA: Berkeley, 1967.

Beauman, Fran. *The Pineapple: King of Fruits*, London: Vintage, 2006.

Benford, Gregory and Malartre. Elisabeth. *Beyond Human-Living with Robots and Cyborgs*, 2007.

Brillat-Savarin, Jean. *The Physiology of Taste*, New York, Alfred A. Knopf, 1971.

Blumenthal, Heston. *The Big Fat Duck Cookbook*, London, Bloomsbury, 2008.

Brown, Jared and Miller, Anistatia. *Spirituous Journey, A History of Drink, (Book One: From the Birth of Spirits to the Birth of the Cocktail)* UK: Mixellany Limited, 2009.

Brown, Jared and Miller, Anistatia. *Spirituous Journey, A History of Drink (Book Two: From Publicans to Master Mixologists)* UK: Mixellany Limited, 2009.

Cowen, Ruth. *Relish*, London: Weidenfeld & Nicolson, 2006.

Child, Julia. *Mastering the Art of French Cooking*, New York: Random House, 2006.

Dalí, Salvador. *Les Diners de Gala*, New York: Felice, Inc., 1973.

Dauncey, Elizabeth. *Poisonous Plants*, London: Kew Publishing, 2010.

Davidson, Alan. *The Oxford Companion to Food*, Oxford: Oxford University Press, 1999.

Edwards, John (et al.) "The influence of eating location on the acceptability of identically prepared foods." *Journal of Food Quality and Preference*, 14 (8) pp. 647-652, 2002.

Embury, David A. *The Fine Art of Mixing Drinks*, New York: Mud Puddle Books, Inc, 2008.

Fernandez-Armesto. *Food: a History*, London: Macmillan, 2001.

Fisher, Len. *How to Dunk a Doughnut: The Science of Everyday Life*, London: Weidenfeld & Nicholson.

Henderson, Fergus. *Nose to Tail Eating*, London: Macmillan, 1999.

Horwitz and Singley (eds.) *Eating Architecture*, Massachusetts Institute of Technology, 2004.

Huysmans, J.K. *Against Nature*, transl. by Robert Baldick Harmondsworth: Penguin Books, 1976

Kelly, Ian. *Cooking For Kings: The Life of Antonin Careme the First Celebrity Chef*, London: Short Books, 2003

Kessler, David A. *The End of Overeating: Taking Control of the Insatiable American Appetite*, Emmaus: Rodale, 2009

Katz, David S. *The Occult Tradition*, London: Pimlico, 2007.

Langan, Peter. *A Life with Food*, London: Bloomsbury, 1990.

Lynn, M. "Determinants and consequinces of female attactiveness and sexiness: Realistic tests with restaurant waitresses." *Archives of Sexual Behavior*, 38, pp 737-745, 2009.

MacDonogh, Giles. *A Palate in Revolution: Grimod de La Reyniére and the Alamanch des Gourmands*, London: Robin Clark, 1987.

Mario, Thomas. *The Playboy Gourmet*, Chicago: Playboy Press, 1971.

McGee, Harold. *McGee on Food & Cooking: an Encyclopedia of Kitchen Science, History and Culture*, London: Hodder and Stoughton, 2004.

Montagné, Prosper et al. *Larousse Gastronomique*, Santa Cruz de Tenerife: Hamlyn, 1961.

Oliphant-Fraser, Jean. *The Champagne Diet*, London: Robert Hale Ltd, 1991.

Pépin, J. *Jaques Pépin's Complete Techniques*, New York: Black Dog & Leventhal Publishers, 2001.

Pleij, Herman. *Dreaming of the Cockaigne: Medieveal Fantasies of the Perfect Life*, Colombia University Press, 2001.

Point, Fernand. *Ma Gastronomie*, New York: The Rookery Press, 2008.

Price, Mary and Vincent. *A Treasury of Great Recipes*, United States of America: Ampersand Press, 1965.

Retzinger, Jean P. 'Speculative visions and imaginary meals', *Cultural Studies*, 22:3-4, 369-390, 2008.

Roberts, C. and Robinson, S.P. "Alcohol concentration and carbonation of drinks: the effect on blood alcohol levels," *J. Forensic Leg. Med.* 14(7), 398, 2007.

Roussin, Rene. *Royal Menus*, London: Hammond, 1960.

Shopsin, Kenny, *Eat Me: The Food and Philosophy of Kenny Shopsin*, New York: Knopf, 2008.

Silverstone, Sally, *Eating In: From the Field to the Kitchen in Biosphere 2*, Oracle: The Biosphere Press, 1993.

Steingarten, Jeffrey. *It Must've Been Something I Ate*, New York: Vintage Books, 2003.

Strong, Roy. *Feast: a History of Grand Eating*, London: Jonathan Cape, 2002.

Thompson, Hunter S. *Fear and Loathing in Las Vegas*, London: Flamingo, 1993.

Warner, Jessica. *Craze: Gin and Debauchery in an Age of Reason*, New York: Random House, 2003.

Whiting, Sydney, *Memoires of a Stomach* London: W.E. Painter 1853.

Young, Carolin. *Apples of Gold in Settings of Silver*, New York: Simon & Schuster, 2002.

Websites

www.case-medicine.co.uk (Centre for Altitude, Space and Extreme Environment Medicine)

www.cookedbooks.blogspot.com (Rebecca Federman, NY Public Library culinary archive)

www.cookingissues.com (Dave Arnold, French Culinary Institute, NY)

www.ediblegeography.com (Nicola Twilley, food writer)

www.historicfood.com (Ivan Day, food historian)

www.psycho-gourmet.blogspot.co.uk (Geoff Nicholson, writer)

www.jellymongers.co.uk

SALUTE

First published in the United Kingdom in 2012 by PAVILION BOOKS
10 Southcombe Street, London W14 0RA

An imprint of Anova Books Company Ltd

Text © Sam Bompas and Harry Parr, 2012
Design and layout © Anova Books, 2012
Photography © Anova Books, 2012, except where indicated otherwise (see Picture Credits)

The moral right of the authors has been asserted.

Commissioning editor: Emily Preece-Morrison
Designers: Georgina Hewitt and Will Ricketts
Special photography: Beth Evans and Nathan Pask
Stylist: Sophie Brown
Copy editor: Kathy Steer
Indexer: Patricia Hymans

ISBN: 978 1 86205 938 2

A CIP catalogue record for this book is available from the British Library.

Colour reproduction by Dot Gradations Ltd, UK
Printed and bound by 1010 Printing International Ltd, China

www.anovabooks.com

10 9 8 7 6 5 4 3 2 1

Finally, a toast to all those who have made this grand adventure possible. Parents, families, friends and lovers who cheered us on from the start. Your unfailing support has been absolutely righteous.

A hearty cheer for all at Anova Books for their skill and panache in realising the book. To Emily Preece-Morrison and Georgie Hewitt, who have steadily piloted it through its course and made it magical. To Polly Powell, who has given us the chance to realise our wildest culinary dreams on the page.

Our literary agent Isabel Atherton of Creative Authors is a champion, honorable thanks.

We've been incredibly lucky to work with most excellent photographers and illustrators. Beth Evans whose skill transforms any spread into a 17th century Dutch Master's painting. Nathan Pask, a titan of graphic photography and monster colour. Andrew Stellitano who happily combines the talents of chef and photographer, Ryan Hopkinson, Jo Duck. And stylist Sophie Brown who enchanted the whole show. The illustrators Boris Vallejo and Julie Bell who have helped us realise wild feasting fantasies.

For this book we asked some of the most inspirational folk we know to contribute text. Thanks to Robin Fegen whose devilling gave the book an indomitable momentum. Your imagination opens our doors of perception. It is brilliant to be able to feature words and images from one of the best directors of feasts we know: Fiona Leahy. You are a constant inspiration.

To Harrods, LSA International and Lladro for generously lending a fleet of crystal, porcelain architecture and assorted chalice. To Daniel Hammond for popping down with his snakes and to Lumiere studio for putting up with live animals, food and explosions over the course of the shoot. To Andaz Hotel who let us use their mysterious Masonic temple.

The greatest thanks to the merry crew of friends and co-collaborators who make every project a joy and pleasure. We are blessed to work with you. To Ann Charlott Ommedal who can design 15 products in a day and shoot them all gloriously, Olivia Bennett who taught us things we never knew were possible with jellying. Special thanks to Beth Adams, Nick Westby, Hugo Richardson, Dom James and Erris de Stacpoole. You've been in it to the hilt. Raising a bumper cup overflowing with mead in your direction.

To the friends and customers who visit our installations and feasts. Who would have thought five years of non-stop fun would culminate in this book. We give you all our gratitude.

If your name's not down it's because one too many feasts have left aching gaps in our memories. The list of people to thank gets longer with every project. Your help is humbling and we offer our sincerest apologies. It is an honour to work with you.

Finally to our heroic girlfriends; we salute you. Love to Cecilia Carey, always and forever. To Emma Rios, brain extraordinaire and stalwart ally and maker, thanks for the illustration and bonus styling.

Raising a glass to feasts of the past, present and future...

PICTURE CREDITS

The authors and publishers would like to thank the following for providing photographs/artwork:
Beth Evans: front cover & pp.22, 23, 25, 27, 32, 40, 46, 49, 52-64, 67-83, 87-93, 100-111, 156-177, 181, 196-204;
Nathan Pask: back cover & pp.2, 31, 37, 50, 84, 95-8, 112-129, 132-139, 150, 151, 179, 212-215;
©: Endpapers: **Jo Duck**; pp. 5, 8b, 9b, 10-11, 66, 131, 155: **Ann Charlott Ommedal**; p.7: **Boris Vallejo and Julie Bell**; p.8t: **Mischa Haller**; p.9t: **Valerie Bennett**; p.13: **Illustrated London News Ltd/Mary Evans**; pp.14-15: **Bettman/Corbis**; p.16: **Private Collection/The Bridgeman Art Library**; p.17: **Archives Charmet/The Bridgeman Art Library**; pp.18-19: **The Stapleton Collection/The Bridgeman Art Library**; p.21: **Illustrated London News**; p.26: **Matthew Andrews**; p.29: **Ann Charlott Ommedal/ Chalice by Maud Trahon**; p.35: **Fiona Leahy**; pp.38, 39, 42, 43 **Ryan Hopkinson**; p.45: **James Loveday**; p.47: **Dan Price**; pp.140, 144, 146, 149, 153: **Ann Charlott Ommedal/ Illustration Emma Rios**; pp.182-195: **Andrew Stellitano**.

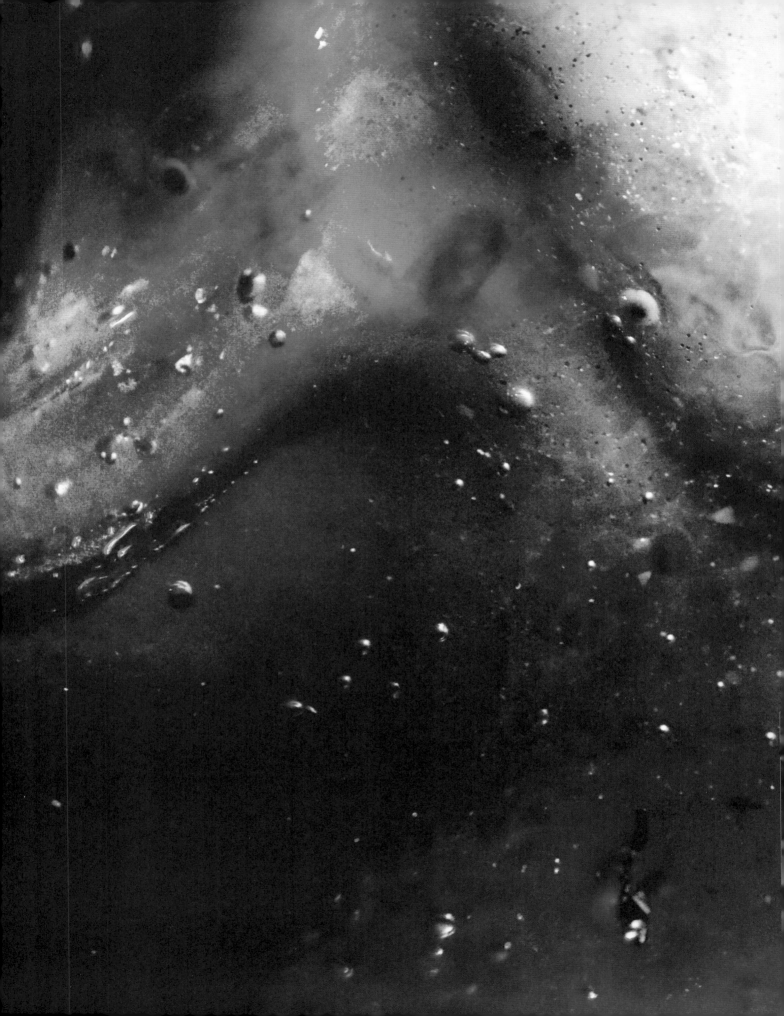